Soul of an Entrepreneur
Book One: Selling H.E.L.L. in Hell

Author: Gino Arcaro
Website: www.ginoarcaro.com
email: gino@ginoarcaro.com

Jordan Publications Inc.
Canada

Editor: Matthew Dawson
Design: Shelley Palomba

Arcaro, Gino, 1957
ISBN 978-1-9278511-0-4
http://www.ginoarcaro.com
Printed in Canada

Gino Arcaro's Story

I started lifting as a dysfunctional 12-year-old, trying to overcome my obesity. Lifting tran formed my life physically and mentally. I have been lifting for over 43 consecutive years, 100% natural. I lift almost every day. It's part of who I am and it will always be, but it doesn't define me.

At 18, I started my policing career. A few years later, I became a SWAT team officer and then at the age of 26, a detective. At the same age, I accepted the head coach position at a high school, a decision that began a lengthy volunteer coaching career. I wrote my SWAT No-Huddle Offense and Defense manuals, (and recently published them) explaining the systems I had created and refined throughout 40 seasons of coaching football at the high school, college and semi-pro levels.

After 15 years, I left policing to teach law enforcement at the local college. During the next 20 years, I became a bestselling academic author, writing 6 law enforcement textbooks that are used in colleges throughout Ontario. Also during that time, I earned a Master degree, an undergraduate degree, and Level 3 NCCP Coaching certification. Then, in 2001, I opened a 24-hour gym called X Fitness Welland Inc. The gym continues to enjoy success in its second decade of operations. eXplode: The X Fitness Training System is a book I wrote that explains my workout system, based on 40+ years of lifting.

In 2010, I left teaching to make the literary transition to motivational writer. My first book, Soul of a Lifter was published in 2011. Since then, I've added several books. Blunt Talk is the name of a series I'm writing dealing with everything from fat loss to interrogation. Soul of an Entrepreneur is another series written to enlighten business owners – current and potential. In the series, 4th and Hell, I tell "David vs Goliath" tales about my Canadian club football team playing in the United States. When my first granddaughter was born, I wrote, Beauty of a Dream and the following year, I wrote Mondo piu Bello to commemorate the birth of her cousin.

I am motivated in my writing by my belief that we all have a potential soul of a lifter. We are called to lift for life. We can lift ourselves. We can lift others.

Keep lifting,
Gino Arcaro

About the Book

H.E.L.L.: **H**eavy **E**xtreme **L**aborious **L**ifting.

Selling H.E.L.L. in hell basic timeline:
Fear less, do more…

- The difference between following your calling and letting your calling follow you is the courage of your convictions.
- The courage of your convictions is your calling speaking as the nagging inner voice that starts from your soul, goes through your conscience, and aims straight for the heart.
- The more your calling chases you, the more you chase your calling.
- The more you try to escape your calling, the more your true self escapes you.
- The more your true self escapes you, the farther you distance yourself from what you're supposed to do.
- The farther you distance yourself from what you're supposed to do, the less chance you'll become what you're supposed to be.
- If you never become what you're supposed to be, you will never fully control your life.
- If you never fully control your life, your destiny is owned by someone else.
- If someone else owns your destiny, you will lead someone else's life.
- If you lead someone else's life, you substitute, replace, and settle for less.
- When you settle for less, you become unsettled.
- When you become unsettled, you suffer a crisis of conscience.
- When you suffer a crisis of conscience, you search your soul.
- When you search your soul, you discover.
- When you discover, you recover.
- When you recover, you re-define yourself.
- When you re-define yourself, you raise your level of consciousness.
- When you raise your level of consciousness, you see what you never saw.

- When you see what you never saw, you will do what you've never done.
- When you do what you've never done, you lose your fears.
- When you lose your fears, you gain control of your life.
- When you gain control of your life, you impact other lives.
- When you impact other lives, you're in business.
- When you're in business, you fight to survive.
- When you fight to survive, you separate from the rest.
- When you separate from the rest, you make things happen.
- When you make things happen, your soul is at peace.
- When your soul is at peace, you shine.
- When you shine, darkness lights up.
- When darkness lights up, you see what others can't see.
- When you see what others can't see, the very best comes out.
- When the very best comes out, the very worst can't get in.
- When the very worst can't get in, you're back in business.

Nothing just happens.
You choose to win.
You choose to lose.

Fear less, do more – A secret to starting your own business from scratch, the secret to staying in business, and the secret to selling H.E.L.L. in hell.

Keep it in mind. Surviving entrepreneurship is all in the mind.

∞

Insights don't just happen.
Insights happen when you turn your sights inside.
Reality teaches the best insights, but you have to look inside to find them.

This series is an insider's look into one soul of an entrepreneur and how his businesses survived selling H.E.L.L. in hell.

∞

Prologue
Won one.

I wrote this series for three reasons:
1. I've been asked a lot about business advice.
2. Being a business owner is the toughest job I've ever had.
3. I'm tired of reading the same old business bullshit that has no relevance to my reality.

My business series is extremely unconventional. It's another soul-searching exercise that challenges popular myths. I'm trying to update my business playbook like I did with football. In my rookie season as a high school head coach in 1984, I went to a football coaching clinic. I used that pro team's playbook. Hell happened. Instead of win-win, we won one. Winning one game out of eight is hell. Burning hell. The one game we won was a product of divine intervention. We didn't deserve to win that game either. I would much rather have gone winless because:
• We deserved it
• Zero is an even number.
• It would have made a better story, because the next year we went undefeated. 10-0 championship.

There were two main reasons for the turnaround:
1. I started my own system. The pro playbook that I learned had zero relevance to my team. None whatsoever. It was an act of insanity to believe that a pro playbook had any relevance to a hapless, hopeless highs school program that had never won anything ever.
2. Lifting. My team was iron deficient. Weak. Weak bodies, weak minds. My team starting a 365 lifting program – year-round.

I romanticize the past. Just last week I told a fairy tale to a gym member about the past. He asked me how football was going. I said, *"Man, kids today are lazy. They're F'd up zombies addicted to Facebook, video games, and Tweeting. Man, it's F'd up today. My team won't lift like they used to. Never had this problem before.* " What a foolish statement. In 1985, we won an undefeated championship with only 26 players. That's it. That's all who stuck it out. At the end of our first week in pre-season, I was urged by two people to fold the team because it looked hopeless. It was a lost cause. That was 26 years ago. When we didn't lift the year before, our roster was packed with 51 players…but we lost. When work had to be done, they cut themselves. There were no cell phones and no internet to blame. It was the same then as it is now. The more things change, the more things stay the same. Hardcore 365 commitment to lifting in football was the same in 1985 as it is now.

My 1985 system evolved into the most unconventional football system and ideology in the world. That's a bold statement, but it's true. I don't have conventional playbooks on offense or defence. The offense is connected to the defence. The offense is an extreme limitless passing machine that operates at warp-speed, one play every 8 seconds, with the build built at the line of scrimmage using a decision-making model. Oh, and I don't kick. We go for it. Always, anywhere, any time.

I never have and never will see what's so complicated about one guy throwing a football to another guy and having other guys block for that guy. I don't see the complexity of telling 11/12 guys to chase the guy who's holding the football and then knock him down. And I never have and never will understand the greatest contradiction of all – not going for it despite all the tough-talk bullshit that coaches pile up about character, adversity, and all the real-life hell that happens away from the insular artificial world of football. If coaches truly had balls, they would not have turned football into the game that so many like to dislike: soccer. I never have and never will understand the appeal of the guy wearing the cleanest uniform kicking the ball over the heads of the guys they couldn't get through. One side tries to move a football forward across a line. The other guys try to stop it. The only issue really is who has the bigger balls, and who stays stronger longer. That's what it boils down to. Biggest balls, stronger longer. It doesn't matter how smart you are, how much money you have, how pretty you look, and how big your stadium is; no balls, no strength – no winning.

My football system is not a conventional playbook. I never have and never will understand the conventional wisdom of expecting players who are starting from scratch to memorize hundreds of pages of Xs and Os diagrams and then try to recall them when the shots are flying for real. My system is limitless. There's no restraining playbook. It's a system about basics, fundamentals, out-working, decision-making under pressure, and pressuring the other team until they break. That's also what my business series is about. It's a non-conventional playbook. It's a simple limitless system that solves real-life problems if you spill you guts by executing to perfection... especially when you think you can't go on.

Xs and Os don't win in football, and they don't win in business. The difference between winning and losing in football is the exactly the same as the difference between winning and losing in business: who has the biggest balls, and who lifts the most.

∞

Chapter 1
Crossing patterns: X–R–Size your freewill.

In 1985, I had to find a word and symbol that represented *limitless*. I needed a simple sign of unlimited potential for a limitless system that promoted limitless growth. I didn't find the answer. The answer found me.

During practice in my second year as a high school head football coach, also in 1985, I realized that the perfect pass play was *crossing patterns*. There was nothing simpler, and the play was unstoppable. It was the simplest yet most dangerous pass play. Two receivers lined up away from each other on opposite sides of the ball. They slant toward each other and then sprint at thirty degree angles until they cross and continue sprinting on their original paths, each going their separate ways to the same higher level. I crossed my arms in front of my chest and said to the quarterback, "X is the new signal for the play called *crossing patterns*. When I cross my arms, I'm calling the *crossing patterns*. X is easy to remember. It's an overhead view of the crossing patterns. Two V's inverted. The bottom shows two receivers lined up wide, away from each other. The bottom of the X is an upside-down V – the starting points of where they are, but not where they're supposed to end up. The middle of the X is the point where they cross paths. That's where an impact is made and things change. The receivers switch sides, and they are guaranteed to outrun the competition. It happens every time. After they cross, the shape changes. The upside-down V turns into an upright V. When I see a V, I see growth. The space in the upright V grows wider, and the lines kept reaching to a higher level. If it works, I will call it again, and again, and again. When you stack one X on top of another, there's no limit to what you can do. The growth is unlimited."

It worked.

The crossing patterns became unstoppable. When we stacked them up by calling the same play, we marched downfield and scored each time. Then I named two positions X, one on offense, and one on defence to represent unconventional positions, that is, multidimensional positions that could line up in unlimited formations to form limitless plays simply by connecting basic strategic *concepts*. There was nothing to memorize and no encyclopedic playbook. A simple limitless system replaced thousands of plays that had to be memorized and recalled. There was no script, just a simple language and decision-making model. A general plan and adaptation: strategize and improvise.

It worked.

Then, I used X to name my workout system. Instead of thousands of pages of scripted workouts, a simple limitless system connected basic strategic *concepts*. Limitless capacity by using a language and simple decision-making models.

It worked.

I named my brand new gym X Fitness. I named my new football team the X-Men. The reason was perception. When I see X, I see hope. I see limitless potential. I see an unstoppable force. I see two crossing patterns that start wide apart, cross paths, make an impact, and then stretch to the next level. I see a wide gap at the bottom that closes as the two stems of the X cross paths in the middle; the point of impact where things change and where the transformation starts. I see the upside-down V transform to an upright V. When I see V, I see growth. I see unlimited growth. I see two paths stretching to the next level. The space inside a V is special – it's the wide open place that keeps growing after two paths cross and an impact is made. The power of X is limitless.

X is a symbol of strength and endurance, a lifelong commitment to athletics and fitness, and a commitment to *never quit*. X is not only our gym's symbol; it's our football team's symbol. It guides us on the field and in the gym. "Never quitting" sounds like a simple concept, but it's not. It's built one rep at a time. X is a promise; a personal pact to stick to it, to fight it out, and to never run from problems. I use X to form limitless systems. I believe that systems can result in limitless growth if two crossing patterns make an impact and stretch to the next level.

X has saved my business's life. After my business started bleeding green, I looked at X and saw a business system. It was a limitless system that worked in my business's reality of selling H.E.L.L. in hell.

We don't cross paths only with who we *want* to meet. We cross paths with who we *have* to meet. Crossing paths starts an exchange where something is taken or left behind. What's taken and what's left behind is the difference between what gets lifted and what doesn't. People don't limit us, we limit ourselves. We all have the soul of a lifter. It's our choice whether we lift and get lifted. That's what this series is about. Lifting or limiting one's self is a choice. It depends on how we X-R-size freewill.

We don't get a choice about who crosses our path, but we have a choice about what to do. We decide whether to drive past or make an impact. You can close your eyes or open them. You can close your heart or listen to it. You can torture your soul or lift it. No one forces you to close your mind, and no one forces you to open it. No one can stop you, and no one can move you unless you cooperate. We make conscious decisions about what to do when we intersect with those who we want to and those we don't. Blown opportunities are the product of those conscious decisions. That's what this series is about. Keep lifting if you want to be lifted.

If people gave us opportunities only if they liked us, we'd all be in big trouble. Trace it back, and you'll find that people lifted us up when we least expected it or deserved it. We are blessed to have had people lift us when we weren't what they wanted. That's what this series is about; soul searching.

Nothing just happens. It wasn't a coincidence that I crossed my arms during football practice in 1985. It wasn't a coincidence that I saw limitless potential in X. Nothing I did afterward was a coincidence, because nothing just happens. I didn't find the solution, the solution found me.

∞

I started high-risk businesses from scratch. I didn't inherit them. I didn't buy them at a discounted rate. I didn't get government grants to fund them. My businesses sell H.E.L.L. in hell. H.E.L.L. is:

Heavy
Extreme
Laborious
Lifting

Not just physical lifting, but mental lifting as well. My businesses sell work – physical and mental exertion. Work is the hardest product to sell, hands down. We (my businesses and team) sell H.E.L.L. in the worst market places – low-income, low-interest places where disposable income is low, and the interest in spending it on H.E.L.L. is even lower. The odds are stacked. They always have been, and always will be.

However, we found a solution; literally and figuratively. We designed a *limitless system* to turn H.E.L.L. into a solution. No one will buy H.E.L.L. unless they believe it's a solution to a problem.

∞

Chapter 2
Solve more than you cause.

- Solve more conflict than you cause.
- Solve more problems than you cause.
- Solve more hell than you cause.

The way to solve more than you cause is through a limitless system made up of two concepts:

1. The concept of positive identification.
2. The concept of the E-soul – the soul of an entrepreneur.

∞

Chapter 3
You can't solve a mystery without positive identification.

"Marks, scars, tattoos?"

Policing taught me the importance of *positive identification*, that is, pinpointing exactly who someone is with speed and absolute certainty. Proving positive ID without a shadow of a doubt is the central focus in every investigation. It doesn't matter how thorough an investigation is, the case crumbles if there's any doubt about ID. Positive identification is the front of the chain. If there is any weakness, the chain breaks. The same applies to business.

We had to ask an arrested person for *marks, scars, and tattoos* to enter the information into the system for future use. IN cases of mangled unrecognized dead bodies, we needed more: dental records, DNA testing, or fingerprints; something unique that branded the person to prove unmistakable identity. Or, someone had to point and say the magic words: *"That's him/her."* You can't solve a mystery without establishing identity first. The same principle applies to business.

Making a profit in a new business is a life-and-death mystery. If your new business doesn't mysteriously stop bleeding green, it gets awarded the dash on the tombstone; the dash between two dates. To avoid the dash, a business needs to build and maintain a strong pulse to keep it alive. A strong heartbeat depends on the *concept of positive identification*, a dual-meaning concept:
- *Easily, quickly, accurately, and continuously* being picked out of a crowd, the fundamental principle behind the lifeline of business: customer recruitment and retention.
- Instant recognition for *positive impact* – positive performance, positive result, positive change, and positive transformation.

Positive identification is 100% recognition of what the business is and where it can be found. It's 100% certainty that the business will deliver the very best solution; a solution to an inner conflict, a solution to a lingering problem, and even an escape from hell. Positive ID happens when a customer automatically recognizes your business from the rest, that it's positively a winner, and selects it by exercising free will and deciding to buy your solution.

∞

Chapter 4
The power of the E-soul.

There are a number of things I completely believe in:
- I believe in the soul of an entrepreneur.
- I believe that the E-soul is real and it won't mislead you.
- I believe the soul of an entrepreneur is a calling, not a choice.
- I believe that the E-soul is not an option to start a business from scratch.
- I believe in guardian angels. I believe that guardian angels and the E-soul work as part of a team that makes calls, protects us, forces us to make calls, and doesn't give up even if they realize they're coaching lost causes.
- I believe the team makes things happen, and we decide how to respond. They call the play, we decide how to execute it. We decide whether to fulfill our assignment or pass it off. We decide whether to give a half-assed effort or give it our very best.
- I believe that we are messaged to fulfill each assignment we're call upon to achieve.

All we have to do is open our eyes so we can see inside our soul and let our heart tell us what to do. But that's easier said than done…

Our businesses should be dead. They're not. They're alive. A series of connected events led me to solutions for problems that were killing our businesses, including a bombardment of self-inflicted attacks. Selling H.E.L.L. in hell is a problem-solving job; a profession that demands making an impact on other people's lives every single day in order for the business to survive. *The only way to sell H.E.L.L. in hell is to help others escape their personal hell.* For me to believe that I escaped business hell on my own exceeds arrogance and ignorance. My team called crossing patterns. Like at every defining moment of my life, I crossed paths with people I wanted and people I didn't want, but I needed them all.

∞

Chapter 5

The power of X.

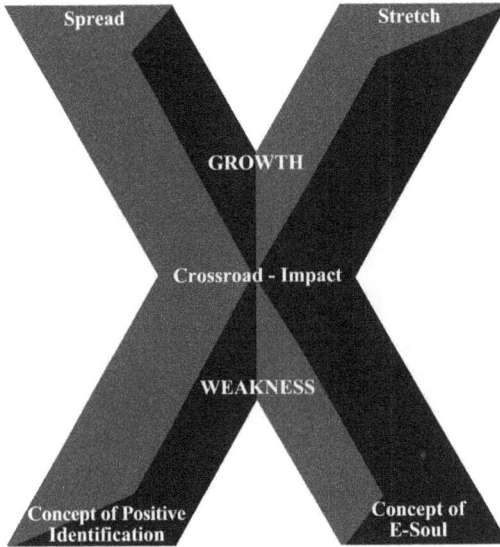

The concept of positive identification and the concept of the E-soul start off miles/kilometres apart. Separated. Disconnected. However, if conscious decisions are made to move them together, they cross paths. When they do, they make an impact that results in limitless growth by stretching your business's performance and spreading the word far and wide. Your business will reach the next level. Then, repeat to get even higher.

∞

Chapter 6
Life-and-death decisions.

Making a profit is an outcome of *decisions* – the customer's and yours. How freewill is exercised determines whether your business lives or dies. If you and customers make the right call, you make a profit. If you don't, you won't. Customer play-calling is a key to business success. Customer play-calling depends on yours. The call you make determines the calls customers make. They're connected. The right calls won't just happen. Customers don't just decide to select your business, your product, or your service. You have to make it happen. If your decisions can't influence customer decision-making, you'll be out of business.

Making a profit depends on a seamless path of customer selection, a continuous flow of customer decisions that choose your solution to escape their personal hell. A chain of decisions based on a chain of events. A chain of customer decisions based on chain of your decisions. They are all connected conscious decisions part of a complex series of calls that are made by customers trying to escape one hell, and a business owner trying to prevent another hell.

You control the chain of events allowing you to influence the chain of decisions.

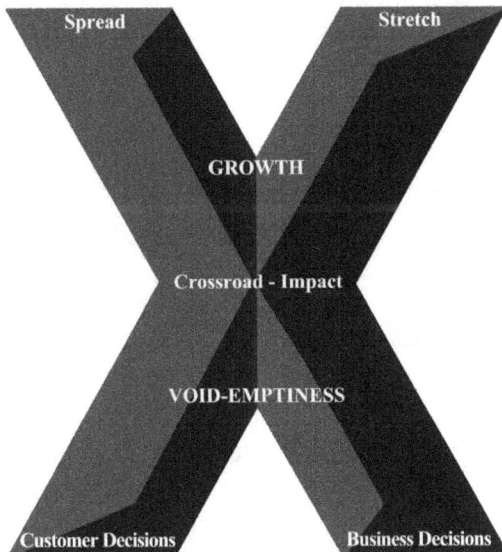

23

Customer decisions and business decisions start off miles/kilometres apart. The gap is a void of emptiness. Conscious decisions move customers and business toward each other so that they're on a crossing-pattern course. When they cross, an impact is guaranteed. If it's a positive impact, the customer *and* the business grow. They're lifted to the next level. Their performances stretch, and the good news spreads. Then the cycle repeats, and the business retains the customer(s). However, if the impact is negative, conscious decisions are made to disconnect downward, returning to a state of separation.

∞

S/he who solves conflict best finds peace. S/he wins big, and ends up in first place. Business and potential customers share the same challenge – conflict. Perception is the secret to any challenge. How we view a challenge determines whether we crush it or it crushes us.

The biggest conflict that business and potential customers share is becoming who we want to be, who we need to be, and who we're *supposed* to be. The gap between what we are and what we want to be causes psychological warfare. Businesses and potential customers are in it together – they're on the *same* team.

Building any team in any field to win a championship takes three basic components that we're supposed to be taught while growing up:
1. Basic human decency.
2. Integrity – honesty out, honesty in.
3. Low self-interest, meaning shift the spotlight.

Coaching football taught me that this simple formula boils down to one word: *conscientious*. A strong conscience wins in any field – sports, business, or any profession. It's impossible to finish in first place with a weak conscience. It won't happen. Appealing to the conscience is a secret to leadership, and the key to achieving sustainable motivation. A new business with a strong conscience is guaranteed to survive a ruthless business Darwinism that kills off businesses without one.

Conscientiousness not only wins championships, it builds the *perfect season*. The conventional definition of *perfect season* is an undefeated record – all wins, no losses. After experiencing the thrill of achieving *perfect seasons*, and the misery of imperfect seasons, I re-defined the term perfect season and discovered a secret to business success – a perfect season is when *sacred memories* are built. Sacred memories build a network of lasting connections that wins the most important business fight of all: customer recruitment and retention.

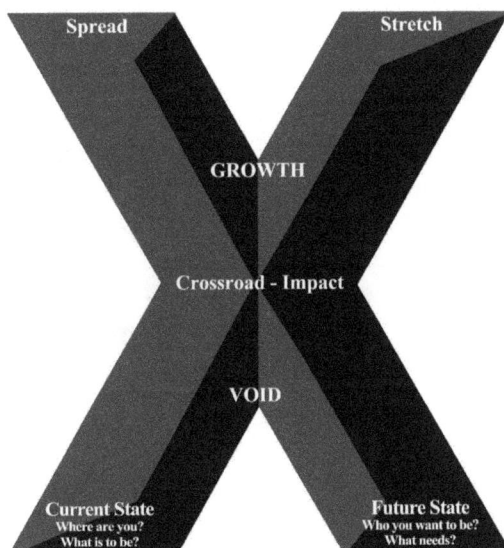

What is and what will be are two paths that have to cross in order to make an impact. Our current state and our future state are separated. The distance depends on where we are at this moment. Crossing patterns are a series of moments that move toward each other. When they cross, an impact is guaranteed to happen. What is not guaranteed is the type of impact and the direction it sends us. Whether we move to the next level higher, or next level lower depends on our level of consciousness – whether we lift it or drop it.

∞

Chapter 7
Soul on fire: The law of call and effect.

"Be who God meant you to be and you will set the world on fire."
– St. Catherine of Siena

∞

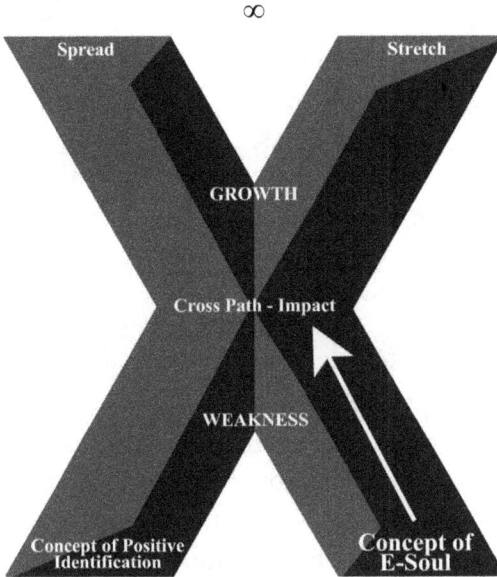

No business is immune from hell. I believe that the power of the E-soul will power your business by leading it to escape the hell that it will positively face. I believe the soul of an entrepreneur is a power source that will light your soul on fire through the dark moments that businesses will experience without fail. The key is to not fail when it happens. Every time the E-soul powers you through hell, you get stronger and smarter. Hell has its purpose – to challenge us, to test our will, to test our strength, to test our smarts, to test our stamina, and to make us tougher. It's impossible to develop the fighting skills needed to survive in a self-generated business without facing hell, without standing up to hell, without fighting hell, and without escaping it.

Escaping the worst brings out our best. Preventing the worst nightmare makes dreams come true. Stopping what you fear the most will make what you want the most to happen. Preventing the worst is the strongest inner drive. It's a force of nature. It's the power of sustainable motivation.

It's a mistake to underestimate the power of the E-soul. The soul of an entrepreneur is part of a team that won't accept losing. All you have to do is get the right call.

∞

Entrepreneurship was not in my blood. I never grew up dreaming of owning my own business. I didn't inherit a business, or business-sense, or even the desire to go into business. Entrepreneurship is not in my DNA, or my genes, or my upbringing. No one ever steered me toward business. My parents were the polar opposites of entrepreneurs. They were illiterate immigrants who survived and escaped the hell of abject poverty and misery in war-torn Italy. They brought with them a boatload of play-it-safe beliefs. Get a factory job, feed your family, pay your taxes, go to church, don't do anything stupid, collect a pension, retire, then die. Taking chances was what other people did. Not us. I was taught conformity. I was taught to blend into the mainstream, assimilate into the crowd, disappear in a traffic jam, and not to stick out. Think the same, look the same, drive the same car, live in the same house, walk the same line, and don't cross it. I was additionally taught the golden rule: don't fuck around. God have mercy on your soul if you fucked around at work, school, or anywhere else.

Owning my own business was never the subject of any what-do-you-wannabe-when-you-grow-up essay. Nothing was. I lied on each one just to get teachers off my back. I scribbled down careers, none of which I can remember, handed them in, and resumed my natural state of confusion. After I legally became an adult, I still had no idea what I truly wanted to do when I grew up…and I still don't. Instead, I was a product of *call and effect*.

I've experienced what is conventionally called *career changes*; radical moves all leading to self-generated businesses that sell H.E.L.L. in hell. I don't call them career changes. Never have and never will. I use three different terms: *following a calling, growing, and escaping hell* – the three elements of *call and effect*. All three are connected. I believe with all my heart and mind that our soul has a calling branded on it. A big picture calling made up of piece-by-piece callings. I believe that a calling is a team effort led by the soul to lead us where we're supposed to go and become what we're supposed to be. For some divine reason, callings are not direct calls. They're mysteries that have to be played out, call after call, testing our freewill and our investigative competence to solve the mystery. Answering a call brings peace. Ignoring a call brings on hell. Answering a call brings on growing pains of personal evolution. Unanswered calls bring on the growing pain of inner hell. Call and effect depends on freewill fitness, that is, how well we exercise freewill. Escaping hell led me to selling H.E.L.L. in hell

I believe we are continuously called to make an impact. Each call that's sent in is intended to make an impact on somebody else, but we grow as a direct outcome – the Law of Impact. Making a difference for others makes a difference for you. Not vice-versa. This chain of events can't be interrupted. We can't ignore the next call because it's inconvenient, or a nuisance, or it doesn't fit the pain-free bunker conventionally called the "comfort zone". When the call is not answered, hell happens. Hell works inside-out. I believe that unanswered calls are a main fuel for a burning inner hell that spreads like wildfire into the environment. I believe that unanswered calls burn a hole inside; a psychological void that's used as a landfill site. It becomes an emptiness that we try to fill with waste and garbage. Freewill is expensive. There's hell to pay if you make the wrong call.

Hell is not created equal. Hell has no limits. We can build infinite layers of hell if we try hard enough.[1] I've tried and have become very good at it. I believe that hell is used as a divine strategy to get our attention and get a point across when we don't answer a call. Hell is paradoxical. Hell can strengthen or weaken, depending on what we do, how well we fight it, and how long we stay in it. No motivator is more powerful than the need to escape hell. Doing it is cathartic and therapeutic. It's transformational. It heals the soul. That's how I moved from one profession to the next – call and effect. Calls were made, and I brought on hell by not answering on time. I believe we are called to execute plays that have been divinely

---

1   Tribute to a masterpiece, Inferno. By Dante Alighieri, the 14th century philosopher-poet who envisioned nine layers of suffering in the Inferno, the Italian word for hell.

called, and we can't call them off or call them our own. I believe we have been blessed with the freewill to execute the play that was called, but I also believe with all my heart and soul that wrong calls won't be tolerated. We pay the price for changing the play. Even though it seems we have discretion to call our own plays, I don't believe we have true discretion. We are expected to follow a system, a decision-making model that we don't have discretion over. We've been given the gift of discretionary freewill with conditions – that we use discretion according to the system. We have to follow protocol. It's a way to make us proficient play-callers without causing chaos.

I believe in the power of call and effect because I finally invested time and energy to investigate my past, and I've determined there's no other logical reason why I became what I became, did what I did, and went where I went. None of my job-hirings made sense. I was obese as a child, I had trouble lifting my ass off a couch, but I got hired lifting one hundred and forty pound flour bags eight hours a day as a teenager in a hell-hole that cut over 90% of those who tried. I never wore a police uniform for Halloween. I never played cops and robbers. I never had a picture taken of me wearing police hats. I never read gun magazines. I can't even stand cop movies, but I became a cop. Not once in my life did the thought of being a teacher ever enter my mind. I never took one teaching course, and my personality never came close to fitting the insular, artificial world of post-secondary academics, but I became a college teacher. I never found football challenging. Throwing a football from point A to point B is pointless in the grand scheme of the universe, but I became an obsessed football coach. I detest with all my heart and soul talking about making big muscles. I hold it in contempt. Yet I try every day of my life to make bigger ones. Writing a book had zero appeal for a personality that needs a rush more often than a junkie, but I became a hardcore writer. The thought of running a business was foreign, but I chose the worst kind to start – selling H.E.L.L. in hell. I left each job at the top of my game. Every new job was not on my inner radar screen until the expiry date passed on my old one. I believe there's something more at play than just nature and nurture. *Thy will be done* is my only logical answer.

Callings operate on a code of secrecy. Don't ask and don't tell. Each job was a training ground for the next and the next, leading me to the business of selling H.E.L.L. in hell. I never had a prior obsession for any of my jobs until after I got them. My jobs were the equivalent of highly addictive substances; the pure stuff. Job obsession is paradoxical – passion, intensity, and burning focus are essential ingredients to winning big…but they build tunnel vision. You can miss the next call that's sent in if you're trapped in a tunnel.

∞

If you're thinking of starting a business from scratch, invest time and energy to investigate your past. Find out if business is your calling. Figure out if you have the soul of an entrepreneur. The E-soul is essential; not an option. For your business to survive, the soul of an entrepreneur is the single-most important factor for business success by whatever definition you give it. The E-soul is a power source that will power your business through moments of hell that the business will invariably experience. Don't underestimate it, and don't ignore it. The power of the E-soul is the difference between breaking limits and getting broken by them. There's pressure in every profession I've worked in, but there is none greater than the pressure of a self-generated business. The pressure of business is in the non-negotiable demand to give your very best every minute of every day. No one will protect your business for half-assed mediocrity. But here's the good news: never forget the true power of the E-soul, because every time the E-soul leads an escape from hell, hell becomes less scary. Every escape from hell makes you stronger and smarter. *S/he who escapes hell, conquers it.*

∞

Chapter 8
What the H.E.L.L?

Physical and intellectual lifting is H.E.L.L. – **H**eavy **E**xtreme **L**aborious **L**ifting. Working out and reading are not popular activities used in commercials. Ad campaigns generally are not centered on physical or intellectual exertion. Hollywood doesn't make movies or television shows starring characters who read a lot or lift weights to exhaustion in the seclusion of a gym. Sexy bodies and brains sell, but not how you get there.

∞

Jordan Publications Inc. is different than almost all self-generated businesses in the history of wo/mankind because it was one of the last businesses born in the webless world. It is one of the only publishing companies born under the shadow of an unusual sign: the O-line. The O-line is a line separating the offline and online eras that unleashed an unprecedented power of communication that changed the rules of business survival. J.P. was one of the only businesses in history that had to cross that threshold as an infant during those crucial formative years.

Jordan Publications Inc. has a unique birthday: 1993. It had one of the most turbulent childhoods in recorded business history because J.P. was born offline, but had to grow up online. Before its second birthday, dysfunctionalism surfaced because Jordan was the product of a monstrous generation gap; a cultural abyss dug out by trying to raise J.P. with an old-world mindset in a new-world that becomes old-world in the blink of an eye.

Less than twenty-four months after Jordan Publications Inc. was born, two miracles happened that I had to see to believe. Someone told me that you could send electronic mail with the click of a button on a computer to anywhere in the world within seconds. To me, this was the equivalent of when civilization was told that the earth wasn't flat. I sent my first email, but was skeptical, like conspiracy theorists who believe the first lunar landing was staged in a movie studio somewhere in Hollywood.

Eventually, our staff huddled around an ancient artifact, a desktop computer, all eyes fixed on a slowly rotating globe on the low-def screen until it slowly happened – *connection*. Dial-up connection complete. We were online. I was shown my first website. All I saw was a construction sign reading: *"This is bullshit. It'll never last. This internet thing is a passing fad."*

∞

Law enforcement textbooks have the same sex appeal as toxic waste. The word *textbook* is a synonym for hell. *Textbook* is one of the world's worst brandings – all pain, no pleasure. Overpriced, boring, and connected to monotonous lectures and torturous exams. Textbooks don't make an impact, don't stimulate, and don't make memories. There's seemingly no feeling, no networking, and no return. Textbooks don't make you feel that head-rush that makes you tell other people good things about it and makes you come back for more

∞

The community college market is academic hell, and community college law enforcement programs are the lowest layer of academic hell. Apathy and lethargy drop the purchase and reading of textbooks in dead last place on the list of priorities. Open-admission standards are paradoxical; it allows opportunities to everyone, and it allows terrible waste of those same opportunities

∞

X Fitness Inc. is different than almost all gyms in the history of wo/mankind. It is one of the first gyms born in the 21st century, and its birth-year of 2001 puts it in a small group of self-generated businesses born right smack in the middle of the culture shock era, the time between two seismic events: the internet explosion and the social media explosion.

X Fitness is one of the few businesses in the history of wo/mankind that never experienced the webless world and experienced its first 3 years of infancy *without* Facebook, Twitter, and Youtube. The time between 2001 and 2004 is unprecedented, and may never be replicated again. Businesses born during those three years had to adjust to the virtual uncertainty of the new online world *and* had to adjust even more to another unknown: social media. Change is paradoxical – it forces you to get strong and survive or it weakens you to extinction. There was no template to determine where or how to invest time, money, and energy.

∞

I started two businesses during the largest revolution in history – two eras of unprecedented technology that suddenly shrunk six degrees of separation to one. This shift sparked uncertainty, unpredictability, and the potential of free-falling down the social IQ scale, the capability of plummeting from educated to uneducated, from relevant to irrelevant, from dynamic to dinosaur, and from expert to extinction at the speed of a keyboard depression all too real. Two businesses suffered culture shock, being born and raised at the only time in history when the word *modern* lost its meaning daily, hourly, and sometimes minute-by-minute.

∞

Working out has the same sex appeal as hemorrhoids. Working out is another synonym for hell. Working out is one of the world's worst brands. All pain, no pleasure. Fitness traditionally has operated on the 90-10 rule: 90% of the public won't buy a gym membership or will quit working out. Gyms fight for 10% of the population.

∞

"Before" and "after" photos are supposed to be uplifting; they're supposed to show positive transformation. "Before" pictures are supposed to be painful, and "after" photos are supposed to be pleasurable. Vice-versa is dysfunctional.

If you searched Google Earth for Welland, Ontario, Canada on April 1, 2001, you would see a healthy, vibrant steel city with a "Grand Opening" sign on the front door of X Fitness. Search the same city exactly 10 years later and you will see grey. You will see utter desolation, depression, despair, despondency, crime, hopelessness, and emptiness. Empty buildings, empty hearts, and empty souls.

Welland's decimation after X Fitness opened was unpredictable. It was impossible to forecast that the city would turn into hell within a few years, and it was impossible to predict that a government with limitless resources would open a competitor in a city on life support.

∞

I started a non-profit organization, a club football team that competed in the United States. The singular purpose of the team was to prove to lost causes that they were misled. I wanted to prove to lost-cause student-athletes that the story of David versus Goliath is not a myth. I wanted to give them evidence that their limitations were self-imposed by adopting the beliefs and opinions of others who set a low bar for them. I wanted to give underprivileged high school graduates a second chance to get to the next level – university, pros, or realize their professional vocation. St. Jude became our patron saint.

My strategy was simple: call out Goliath, several Goliaths, and call out our inner beast. But that doesn't just happen. Calling it out will not happen automatically, mystically, or overnight. A heavy price has to be paid. The only way to become the strongest is to play the strongest...*and train accordingly.* We became Canada's only collegiate club team to play in the U.S.A. – a challenge of Biblical proportions.

Football is hell. It's a viscous high-risk, high-impact sport with the potential of catastrophic injury. Coaching football in Canada is another layer of hell, because if the sport is not played on ice, it doesn't count. Iceless sports are counter-culture. Training for football is another layer of hell. It's a Darwinian process that exposes true love, and it separates those who truly love hell and those who love the *thought* of it. However, the deepest layer of hell is lining up against Goliath...unless you've paid the price.

X Fitness sponsored my non-profit football team. The business of making an impact on lives is paradoxical – it can make you or break you. You have to be careful that both businesses don't become non-profit. But, if you play it right, you can learn a secret to business survival: the *sacred memory.*

∞

Jordan Publications Inc. and X Fitness Inc. should be dead, but they're not. They're alive and have survived past the decade mark in hell. We didn't just beat the odds, we had to escape hell and keep escaping the *threat* of more hell. Nothing teaches the truth better than escaping hell. Nothing teaches hardcore lessons better than living it, because escaping hell is the toughest place you will ever have to escape, and it teaches you clock management. Here's phase one, a warm-up of what I've learned through all these seemingly lost causes:

1. ***Conventional thinking will kill your business.***
   The myth of the business plan is just one example. It was impossible to write a meaningful business plan for either business that I started. The 5-year business plan written for Jordan Publications Inc. was irrelevant less than two years later because the language was foreign. Website was not in the dictionary when the business plan was written. Neither was e-mail, Google, or search engine optimization. Friends were those we counted on, not counted up. It's impossible to budget for the unimagined. Cell phones and hypertext designers were science-fiction wants; not needs.

   The X Fitness business plan was ancient within three years. The "economic collapse" of the city was not typed into the business plan...neither was "social media campaign". Six degrees of separation shrunk to one. Instead of the conventional business plan, we developed our own: strategize and improvise. General planning with immediate adaptation to fit the situations. Challenge all conventional business wisdom. Test it before you believe it. Discover the evidence of what works in your reality.

2. ***Separate business myths from fact.***
   Welland is not Los Angeles, Rome, or Tokyo. What works in someone else's reality is not guaranteed to work in yours Challenge all conventional business wisdom. Test it before you believe it. Discover the evidence of what works in your reality.

3. ***Build your own case.***

    Our business reality has its own DNA and its own brand. Do not instantly give credibility to self-professed experts who claim to know the secrets of getting rich quick in all realities. Never immediately award top marks for credibility to any business expert. Make them prove that their advice will work in your reality. S/he who asserts must prove. That was the first sign I read in a police station the day I was sworn in as an 18 year-old. Awarding instant credibility will kill your business. Credibility has to be earned. What works for a fortune for 500 companies may have zero relevance to what works in selling H.E.L.L. in hell. What the latest study about consumer trends reports may have zero relevance in your reality. What your favourite professor or business guru teaches you about business may have zero relevance in your hell. Build your own case. Investigate your reality. Discover the relevant evidence, the truth about what works and what doesn't work in your reality. Challenge all conventional business wisdom. Test it before you believe it. Discover the evidence of what works in your reality.

4. ***Vet the source.***

    Every business will have to escape some layer of hell at some point in time. There's a strong probability that you will search for answers to help you solve the mystery of escaping hell. Your search will likely lead you to a number of self-professed experts – in person or in writing. The first step in the long process of rating a self-professed expert's credibility is a background check. And the first step in the investigation is finding out if the expert has actually escaped hell. Has the expert lived it? Challenge all conventional business wisdom. Test it before you believe it. Discover the evidence of what works in your reality.

5. ***Think outside the box until the box disappears.***

    This does not mean trash conventional wisdom. Far from it. It means change the direction of your thinking – think from outside-in. You can never see outside the box while you're locked inside, but you can see inside and outside the box from outside it. You can also see forever with no box. All boxes are artificial limitations. Challenge all conventional business wisdom. Test it before you believe it. Discover the evidence of what works in your reality.

6. *Build your own system.*

Coaching football taught me two valuable business lessons: The sports model is a key to winning in business, and never, ever borrow a playbook; build your own system. There is zero difference between winning and losing in sports, and winning and losing in business. What wins championships on the field applies in any field…but so does getting clobbered. Winning is a by-product, not a goal…but so is losing. Winning is an outcome of calling one play after another systemically instead of seat-of-the-pants winging it. Winging it won't win it, but borrowed playbooks are misfits that build more misfits. A system is a customized, limitless way of letting your team play the game, compete, and win big. A system is more than a protocol or manifesto, and more than a rigid, inflexible script. A system is a problem-solver. A system is limitless plays and limitless solutions for every challenge, every situation, and every mystery. The secret to building a system is to challenge all conventional business wisdom. Test it before you believe it. Discover the evidence of what works in your reality.

7. *Never ignore the basics.*

Conventional wisdom does include hardcore truths that work. Conventional thinking does include irrefutable, unchallenged building blocks of winning anywhere and any place. They're called the fundamentals. The basics. They're the core of a fundamental human decency and conscientiousness that will build a winner in any field. A secret to finding the basics is to challenge all conventional business wisdom, but not the basics. Test it before you believe it. Discover the evidence of what works in your reality.

∞

Chapter 9
Sustainable motivation: Crossing patterns.

Sustainable motivation is a key to self-generated business survival. It's the switch that unplugs an endless source of inner core strength needed to survive the inevitable threats to a new self-generated business. If you're deciding whether to start a business, or you have already made up your mind, or your business is struggling, I strongly urge you to investigate yourself, and find a source of sustainable motivation that will push you to fight to the death to stop your business from dying instead of pulling the plug at the first sign of blood.

Motivation is not created equal. There are short-term incentives as well as temporary stop-gap measures, and there's sustainable motivation, long-term, hard-wired rocket-boosters that automatically fire when faced with opposing forces. Sustainable motivation is the only defence that will prevent you from not cracking up under the intense pressure of making your own business work.

Here's how I found mine: *"Non permettete a nessuno di prendermi per un pazzo."* A dying declaration. A force of nature and nuture. This is the single-most powerful performance demand a human can make. A dying declaration isn't a multiple-choice test. There's no menu of selections. A dying declaration is a no-brainer… only one choice is given. Failing to comply is not optional. In fact, it's a crime. The wish of a dying man became the blood and guts of my sustainable motivation.

No other human has ever motivated me since, or ever will motivate me more. I don't attend packed arenas, fist-pumping along with a hopped-up motivational speaker. I don't buy motivational CDs. The same tired old motivational books, videos, and speeches have no effect on me. I'm totally immune to the conventional motivational gurus. One statement by a dying man made the biggest impact in my life. It branded into my soul. That one statement influences every thought and action of every day. It has driven me ever since I first heard it. It drives me today, and it will drive me for eternity. It's the source of my inner strength that I plug into whenever I'm tempted to kill valuable clock time with self-pity.

My father was not on his deathbed when he said it, but it was the last meaningful statement he made during a long slow painful death march. *"Don't ever let anyone take you for a fool."* It wasn't a pep-talk. There wasn't a smile, or a slap on the back, or hair-rustling. It came out of nowhere. No words before it…and nothing following it. No smile. No *"Son, let me tell you some good advice."* Not even eye contact. I was just passing by. It was the unmistakable sound of a broken will, a worn-down spirit trapped in a customized hell, but it came straight from the heart.

My father was different than any human I've met, or read about, or watched on the screen. I've never heard a story like his. I've never met anyone like him. He was not Ward Cleaver. He could not read English, couldn't understand more than a hundred English words total, and he couldn't string a proper English sentence together. He could barely read and write Italian. There were no heart-to-hearts, no playing catch in the backyard, no fishing trips, no campfires, no Disneyland, and no vacations whatsoever. I don't remember any other conversation I ever had with him. His entire life was labour. Pound-for-pound. I've never met a stronger, more driven human. He was tireless, and not a person to be fucked with. Publicly, my father was a complete gentleman despite his contempt for assholes and laziness. He never embarrassed himself. I heard him tell only one person to fuck off in English – a stoner who missed the drug dealer's house next door at 2:00 am one night.

My father never sat in the basement playing video games, never posted adolescence on Facebook, never lived his life vicariously through overpaid millionaire athletes and celebrities, and never wasted time chatting on discussion boards. He was too busy working to escape a hell that I have never experienced and never even heard of anywhere else.

I have never endured a fraction of my father's struggle. I have never had to pack up and move around the globe penniless and illiterate, forced to make a living without being able to communicate. I have two university degrees, four diplomas, and half a PhD dissertation done and still can't figure out the world, the people in it, or how to make things work. Somehow, he did. I never saw him read. I never read anything he wrote while he was alive. He flew off the handle when I asked him how far he went in school. Yet, he made it work. No excuses, no complaining, and no whining. He just worked. Until he got sick and lost his work and his inner demons surfaced. Work couldn't contain them any longer. His pain-reliever lost its strength.

"Don't ever let anyone take you for a fool." is the shortest but most compelling autobiography I've ever heard. A life story condensed to a nine-word narrative that explained everything I needed to know. He was passing the torch with his version of a cautionary tale. I got it. I understood exactly what he meant. The clock ran out. The tank was empty. He had worked to failure. He made Henry David Thoreau prophetic – he went to his grave with a song still in his heart. His life had been a portrait of conflict. Inner and outer unresolved conflict. No peace, and no tranquility. He was a tortured soul that couldn't reconcile that he had been taken for a fool. I made a silent pact that day. I took a solemn oath. I made a sacred vow. A promise is a promise. The beauty of a dying declaration is what it grows into. It built my personal, non-negotiable ideology that has become my business plan:

- On Judgment Day, I expect to be asked, *"What did you do with your gifts?"* My goal is to have a good answer.
- Evidence is going to be needed to build a case on Judgment Day. The best evidence I've discovered is to make the biggest positive impact on as many lives as possible, continuously. I've learned that there is no greater reward than putting up ladders for others. I felt it. It made me rich quick where it counts the most – inside. That's my business goal. That's my mission. I want to get even richer quicker deep inside by making others even richer.
- I will never let my potential be controlled by a boss. My destiny will be self-controlled.
- Never again will I let workplace conflict kill the clock. My deepest regret in my life is the amount of time wasted in mind-numbing, soul-killing workplace conflict.

Clock mismanagement. Time killed off the clock that can't be put back. No replays, no reruns, and no repeats.

- I will never fear competition. You get strong by playing against the strongest. Call out Goliaths, and then call out your inner beast.
- I will never let fear of risk block my life. The only risk I fear is the risk of being bored to death and wasting the one life I've been given.
- I will never fear being different. I will challenge every thought I hear and read. I will never be afraid to stand out of a crowd.

Nothing endures without ideological consistency. These seven points form my business philosophy. It worked for me in forty seasons of coaching football. Sports taught me that ideological consistency is the blood and guts of true winning. It taught me success that transcends the scoreboard. Additionally, sports taught me that ideological *inconsistency* leads to losing that transcends the scoreboard. Ideological consistency strengthens the core. Without a solid core, you will bend. When your core softens, you'll break.

∞

I never have and never will use the term *bucket list*. Four reasons why:

1. I don't have the follower-gene. I have a burning passion to be extremely different. I don't want to spend my life as an echo by simply repeating everything I hear. Originality is vitality. When something becomes fashionable like a bucket list, I don't follow.
2. A bucket list is a preparation to die.
3. A bucket list is a replacement for true achievements; a way to fool one's self about living a stimulating life. If you have to list the big stuff, the rest of your life must be pretty dull. *Living it* has to be habitual, not a check mark on a list.
4. Bucket lists are limiting. You can do better than that. Every list has a *false finish line* that gets crossed too early, long before you're actually done. Whatever you write down, you can do more. Guaranteed.

Instead of a bucket list, I have one overriding mission that covers everything I want to achieve: *not to waste my parents' sacrifice.* That's my life mission statement. It's my *limitless system* that fuels my drive more than any scripted bucket list ever could. My parents didn't struggle just to let me live a life of unimaginable comfort in the greatest country on Earth. I have an obligation to make the biggest impact possible. I have a moral responsibility to make the biggest difference I possibly can. Their struggle didn't just happen. It had purpose. It was part of a big picture, a mystery that that goes far beyond what I can envision. I believe all of us are called to advance what our ancestors built. I believe that our lives are not compartmentalized into separate entities, apart from the past and future. Our lives are not isolated from past generations or future ones. Our lives are connected, forming a seamless path that's supposed to lead to growth, betterment, and actualization of those who have, are, and will share Earth. I believe that we are called to move the ball as deep as possible. Wasting sacrifices, that got us where we are, by coasting through life not giving it your very best or not even trying, is a crime against humanity – the worst form of an ungrateful heart[2] and soul.

Anyone can write down lists, and goals, and plans, but getting it done is what counts. I never have and never will believe that writing it down makes a difference. Writing it down will not develop work ethic. Writing it down will not make you need it like you need air. Writing it down won't make you grow some or show some. Writing it down will not make you a great leader. Writing it down will not make you a tireless worker. I don't believe in the conventional wisdom of rigid, inflexible plans and goals. I tried writing down a list of New Year's goals once. I forgot the goals and lost the list. Missing the follower-gene makes it impossible to follow a strict script…even my own. However, I *do* follow opportunities. I believe that opportunities are defining moments that are created for our benefit by our team, whether we expect them or not, whether it

---

2   Tribute to a masterpiece, Core 'ngrato (Sicilian for Ungrateful Heart). Written by Salvatore Cardillo in 1911, Core 'Ngrato has been a timeless classic performed by Italian tenors and made even more famous by Junior Soprano in the finale of The Sopranos season three, called Army of One.

fits our definition of perfect timing or not, and whether they fit our plans and goals or not. I believe that our gift of freewill decides whether the opportunity is a save or blown opportunity. Discretion is the heart and soul of our future. How we respond to what's put in front of us, whether we've planned for it or not, determines what opportunities are missed and which ones are completed. I don't believe that every call can be planned for. *We get the call, we make the call*, and then we live with it or live it.

Every profession, every job, and every defining moment in my career happened from an opportunity that was presented unexpectedly. Not one of my careers happened from a plan I wrote out or a long-term goal. My entire 40-year work and professional career has been the result of *crossing patterns*. Every career start and career change happened because of *crossing paths* with people who I wanted and didn't want, but all of whom I *needed at that moment.* I've questioned some of the calls I've received and some of the calls I've made, but once the play is in the books, it can't be changed and can't be replayed. Just wait for the next call and make the next call. A secret is execution – whatever call you make, carry it out with everything you've got. Bring out you're very best. Make each play count. Even bad calls can score big points if the play is executed to perfection. That's why I replaced bucket lists, scripted plans, and goals with a formula that has worked out in every football season I've coached – the *Rule of Lifting the Bar.*

Lifting the bar is a system of going to the next level, and the next, and the next by constantly raising *minimum performance standards* and passing them with the *Principle of Strategizing and Improvising.* I never have and never will write down a set of concrete goals or concrete plans for any athletic performance – not for football, and not for working out. Concrete goals and concrete plans are limiting. They build a ceiling. We lift the bar every workout, every practice, and every game to build a *minimum standards formula*, a threshold that must be crossed each time. Lifting the bar guarantees moving to the next level…and the next, and the next. There are infinite levels of performance. They're not neatly divided into rookie or veteran. It's impossible to compartmentalize performance into three packages of beginner, intermediate, and expert. Rookies are not created equal, and neither are veterans, beginners, or experts. Minimum standards set the bar. Sustainable motivation lifts. Therein lies part of my business plan: *the connection between sustainable motivation, crossing patterns, getting the call, making the call, and lifting the bar.*

∞

Dying declarations don't just happen. I believe they're another play that's called forcing a call. We have to decide how we play it out. I believe that takes a team effort.

I have exhausted my guardian angel. S/he has saved me from hell repeatedly. My first exposure with my guardian angel wasn't pleasant. My grade one teacher showed us a picture of a kid being followed by her guardian angel. The lesson was spooky and creepy. The guardian angel was described as a micromanaging control freak spying on our every move. Later, I learned about the power of labels…false allegations that can lead us to misjudgment. I figured out that guardian angels can be misunderstood – the product of bad labeling. My guardian angel is like the offense linemen I coach. They have to block attackers hell-bent on busting up the star who will get all the credit. They have to clear paths for the star to score points. Not only that, but they have to remain anonymous. No one knows their names, no one talks about them, and no one gives them any praise. Protection and security without glory. Silent warriors. We don't acknowledge them until the protection breaks down and they let the pressure through. Then there's hell to pay, and we blame them, holler, and point fingers.

I believe guardian angels are part of a team that makes calls, protects us, forces us to make calls, and doesn't give up even if they realize they're coaching lost causes. I believe the team makes things happen, and we decide how to respond. They call the play, and we decide how to execute it. We decide whether to fulfill our assignment or pass it off. We decide whether to give a half-assed effort or give it our very best.

I believe that nothing just happens. Nothing happens automatically, and nothing happens randomly. Policing taught me not to believe in coincidences; just connections. What seems to be a coincidence is actually a connection that has to be figured out; mysteries that have to be solved.

Making money is a necessity for a business owner, otherwise, you'll lose everything you own. But making money will never be a sustainable motivation. Making money is a by-product of sustainable motivation. My goal is to empty the tank – fulfill every fibre of my calling. I'm driven by the fear of wasting life, and the fear of being bored to death. We're not born to be bored. To get there, I will continue to challenge every thought I hear, and every thought I read. That's the only way to find the truth about how to sell H.E.L.L. in *our* hell.

∞

Chapter 10
Starting from scratch:
Mind your own business.

Miraculous.

Deciding to become a full-time business owner turned into a miracle. It saved me from hell. Nothing beats its main benefit-package: *psychological freedom...* intellectual freedom, emotional freedom, and freedom from workplace hell. However, escaping hell is expensive. There's a big price to pay. No discounts, no deals, and no cheap imitations. The price is not only financial. There's an intellectual and emotional price that has to be paid to learn what needs to be done and to do what has to be done. You have to make all the tough calls that need to be made to survive a ruthless business Darwinism that will cut up the weak, the unprepared, and those unwilling to go where very few will venture into. If you start a new business and can't cut, you will burn up in a self-generated living hell. You have to find out if you have what it takes before you make the decision to start a business. If you are unwilling to fight through a natural struggle that new businesses have to undergo, you will get cut from an unforgiving process that refuses to let the weak get to the next level. But the fight is worth it because you're fighting for something that you cannot buy, borrow, or steal – *full psychological control.* Full control of your potential, full control of your destiny, full control of your true calling, and full control of your true self. When I became a full-time business owner, I regained full ownership of my mind, my thinking, and my growth that I thought I had forfeited years ago.

I started three businesses from scratch. Point-Zero. All three with limited resources – financial, human, and physical. Not enough money, not enough staff, and not enough equipment. Bare minimum. One business was non-profit, two for-profit. Soon, all three became non-profit because all three were in the business of *selling H.E.L.L. in hell.* I had plenty of warning. The experts cautioned me that all three were extremely high-risk businesses. All three were the toughest businesses to start and survive in because they were in the business of *selling H.E.L.L. in hell* – **H**eavy **E**xtreme **L**aborious

Lifting, physically and intellectually. A gym, books, and football were my products in the lowest of low-income markets financially, mentally, and physically. My businesses sell physical and intellectual pain and discomfort in painfully uncomfortable economies; places that nose-dived into darkness faster than the speed of light. Lost-cause businesses in lost-cause places until we found-cause.

I never had any problem building winning teams for other people, never had any problem making other people successful, never had any problem bringing out the very best in people, and never had any problem making tough calls that others wouldn't or couldn't make until it was time to do it for myself in my own business…but then I blinked. A stranger moved in and took over my mind. I began acting out of character. I got soft and complacent; the two deadly conditions that made me the highest-risk to my business. I became the biggest threat to business survival. I didn't suddenly forget everything I had learned about winning; I just didn't do it. *There are two leading causes of losing: not knowing enough, and not doing enough.* You can't tell them apart when you get soft and complacent.

Softness and complacency doesn't just happen. Nothing just happens. They develop. They're products of conscious decisions that are voluntarily made. Neither one mysteriously leaves until the mystery is solved and the solution is put into action. I discovered *the solution* before it was too late. A voice from above sent me the answer. Messages are sent to us in mysterious ways. It's very easy to ignore messages from above for a number of reasons – too busy, too angry, too frustrated, too preoccupied, or just plain too stubborn to believe it's actually a message. This life-saver was sent from the least likely messenger, high above football practice in a mechanical lift. A messenger, who I was on the verge of firing from my business and my life, shouted down a life-altering message that struck like *en*lightening – 17 words of enlightenment that saved our business:

"You should run the gym the same way you run a football team. You'd make a fortune!"

Never ignore simplicity. Never ignore the basics. Never look past what you already know. We beat overwhelming odds by *doing what I had learned outside of business.* The coaching model that I used to build winning football teams applied precisely to winning in business. My coaching model had been influenced and shaped by every career I had worked in and every academic degree or diploma I've ever earned. It was the result of a chain of life-experience and academic events. A big price was paid for that education, and an even bigger price was paid for ignoring it. Every secret I needed to know about how to win in business wasn't a secret. I had learned everything I needed to know about how to start a business from scratch. How to run it, how to make it survive and thrive, how to win, and how to win big, but I fell into the biggest trap you can get caught in – complacency. Getting soft. I made the critical mistake of compromising what I believed in and what I knew had worked in the past. I lost myself by ignoring simplicity, by ignoring the basics, by ignoring my heart, and, most of all, by ignoring my soul. Missing and inaction. I had to re-discover myself by investigating failure; studying loss after a crushing defeat until the mystery was solved. Digging deep, I found what was lost.

Self-generated business survival is a slugfest; an economic street-fight. If you don't learn how to survive, your business will get pounded to the ground, beaten into submission, bloodied up, and then dropped from the standings of business competitors. Unless you train consistently, relentlessly, and obsessively, you will be a victim of a merciless, unforgiving business Darwinism that will kill your business prematurely. A self-generated business will not run by itself. It will not raise itself and it will not lift itself. Business survival depends on *fully-invested attention* – strict, undivided, burning, concentrated attention. *What you focus on grows.* What you don't focus on will weaken and die.

∞

Before I became a full-time business owner, I had two choices: work in someone else's hell, or try to sell H.E.L.L. Freewill had to be exercised. It was my choice. No one was forcing me, coercing me, or holding me hostage in someone else's hell against my will.

I voluntarily chose to stay in someone else's workplace long after the alarm went off because of the *power of inducements,* that is, temptations. Over 100,000 temptations annually, plus benefits and a pension. But that wasn't the most powerful force that kept me in workplace hell…not even close. The most powerful forces were *conditioning, comfort,* and *competence.*

Conditioning has paradoxical power – it can make you or break you. It can bring you peace or break you to pieces. There's a clear line between good conditioning and bad conditioning. One makes you grow; the other stunts your growth. One is an escape from hell; the other brings it on. I was conditioned from birth to believe, rightfully, that you should be thankful for any job, shut up and work like a farm animal, give way more than you get, and never ever embarrass yourself by backing down or giving in to struggle. Giving up and quitting was never an option in my conditioning. Fight through your struggles; never flee from them. The problem was that I was never taught the difference between a natural struggle and an unnatural struggle. Struggles are not created equal. Natural struggles are worth it – an immutable part of winning. Unnatural struggles are energy-wasting, soul-killing conflicts that need to be escaped and not fought. Knowing the difference is a secret to professional survival, to peace of mind, to reaching your potential, and to avoiding the dread and regret caused by underachieving. Natural struggle strengthens. It makes you grow. Unnatural struggle weakens. It stunts growth. The problem is that they look almost exactly the same; they both look like hell, sound like hell, and feel like hell. One you have to stick to in order to get anywhere in life, and the other you have to escape from to get anywhere in life. Telling them apart is not easy, but there are clear signs to read. There are messages, omens, and hardcore evidence that prove which is which. Natural struggles light your soul on fire; unnatural struggles simply burn you up.

Comfort has paradoxical power – it can make you or break you. It can bring you peace or break you to pieces. There's a clear line between good comfort and bad comfort. One form of comfort makes you grow; the other stunts your growth. One is an escape from hell, the other brings it on. Every career I've had gave me the opportunity to grow beyond my wildest dreams by challenging myself to face fears that are capable of killing body, mind, and soul. However, each career had expiry dates that I failed to read or conveniently chose to ignore. Oddly, none of my careers had ceilings. Organizations built them…and they kept lowering them. Professions have limitless potential. Winning organizations know how to keep it that way. Losing organizations impose limits.

Becoming very good at what you do has paradoxical power – it can make you or break you. Competence can bring you peace or break you to pieces. There's a clear line between being very good and too good – one makes you grow, the other stunts your growth. Becoming very good at what you do brings the ultimate inner reward of achieving what seemed unachievable for both team and self. But becoming *too* good can build addictions – addictions to approval, to flattery, to praise, and to the safety of risk-free certainty and familiarity. Being *too* good brings addiction to the comfort of a pain-free existence.

I crossed each line. I stayed in professions that I had outgrown, and I stayed in a workplace hell that had to be experienced to be fully believed. I didn't even see the lines, because I was too busy shadow-boxing; fighting no one. I was fighting to change the unchangeable. I learned a harsh lesson – *mind your own business*. If you're going to fight with all your heart and soul, make it count; fight for your own business. Fight for your own team, not someone else's. If you invest the same energy fighting for your own business that you fight for someone else's, you will become filthy rich…even financially rich. *Minding your own business* requires investing your mind fully into your own business. *Mind your own business* means investing the power of your own intellect into your own business instead of someone else's. *Mind your own business* means pouring your thoughts, your creativity, your ingenuity, your authenticity, your heart, your soul, and your guts into *your own business* because *your own business* has no ceiling, no limits, no boundaries, and no box. *Your own business* will not limit you to think or act inside the confines of a tight box. If I had minded my own business, this series would not have been written…or it would be a different story. If I had minded my own business, my businesses would not have struggled unnaturally. If I had minded my own business, I would not have crossed the line.

One of the reasons I stayed in workplace hell was my misguided notion that I could make a bigger impact in someone else's organization instead of on my own. After having made a difference working for other people, I fooled myself into justifying not leaving a workplace that was corrupting my soul with the irrationalization that having made a difference in the past would lead to making a bigger difference in the future. I've been blessed to have worked in professions that give you the capacity to make a big difference – to make repeated long-term impacts that stretch timelessly, but I underestimated two things: the power of organizational control that limits the difference you can make, and the power of a self-generated business which doesn't. If I had minded my own business from the start, I could have made a bigger impact because if you mind your own business, there's no limit to the difference you can make. Minding your own business lets you fully control the size and depth of the impact you want to make. The size of the difference you can make is in your hands, mind, heart, and soul.

∞

I started my businesses, but didn't leave a job that I developed contempt for. I paid the price for ignoring the expiry date – embarrassment and humiliation. I was surrounded by a team that focused intently and intensely on conflict instead of doing what taxpayers paid them incredibly well to do. I was stuck in the middle of an organizational sand fight that can't be described with mere words. As the face of a monstrous money-making program, I was mired in a bizarre de-militarized zone – expected to make peace without the authority to do it. A toothless face-of-the-program. The public rightfully holds the face-of-the-program accountable, but when that title is vacant, when it's empty of any true substance, and when there are no tools and no authority to do what needs to be done to deliver as promised, to deliver the absolute best, to deliver far more than expected, and to deliver far more than you receive, you have two choices: resign or resign. Resign from the organization, or resign yourself to compromise what you believe in with all your heart and soul. Exercising freewill takes extreme fitness; top-notch, next-level strength. You have to invest in yourself by thoroughly investigating which choice to make. The smartest investment you can make is true soul-searching; pure, unabated soul-searching where you question yourself relentlessly and without mercy to find the truth.

You will never discover the truth by asking lame questions, or by rushing it, or by not spilling your guts. You will never spill your guts if you aren't willing to spill your guts. You will never discover the truth until there's just enough pressure that forces you to admit it for your own peace of mind. You will never discover the truth unless you find enough evidence as back-up. You will never find the truth without two-way honesty – honesty out, honesty in; and vice-versa. You get what you throw out: dishonesty out, dishonesty in; and vice-versa. Honesty has paradoxical power – it can make you or break you. It can bring you peace or break you to pieces. There's a clear line between honesty and brutal honesty – one makes you grow, the other can stunt your growth if you cannot accept it. Honesty can be an escape from hell or it can bring it on. It depends on what you're searching for – to get better or to feel better.

Insights don't just happen. Insights don't happen automatically, overnight, or randomly. We make our insights happen, and then we have to discover them. I've tried to rank my business mistakes in order of severity and stupidity, but it's no use. Every time I say *worst business mistake I ever made*, something else takes its place. There's no straight line to the truth. There's no linear path that completes a thorough soul-searching. The reason I made the worst business mistakes in the first place, and the reason I'm discovering them, have to do with self-honesty and the lack of it – self-deception made them, but self-honesty revealed them. Being self-deceptive manifested in irrationality. Illogic. Being honest changed it. I learned the true power of self-honesty while coaching football. It's part of a secret formula for winning – *the science of investigating losing*. Winning is learned by studying losing *in your reality* by studying game film and honestly evaluating every call made, every call not made, and how each play was executed. Find the true weaknesses and strengths, not the perceived ones that are assumed based on what we want to believe.

Solve the mystery of losing by investigating every defeat, and discover hardcore evidence of what specifically caused it. Then, change it. After you win, start another investigation; investigate winning. Study winning to discover the evidence of winning big *in your reality.* Policing taught me the power of evidence. Coaching football taught me the power of evidence *in your reality.* I learned that winning in the pros does not fully apply to where I coach. The pros have elite athletes to work with. I have to make athletes them from scratch. Two different concepts. There's the biggest difference in reality-relevance: level of expertise. The same applies to a self-made business. What applies to a Fortune 500 company does not fully apply to my business. To solve the mystery of what's needed to make my business work I had to study our reality. That's how *true reality insights* are discovered. Experiment, test, research, study it intensely, and thoroughly investigate winning and losing *in your reality.* A thorough investigation of losing uncovers the secret to winning – guaranteed. Then, investigating winning discovers the secret of winning big. *Reality of insights – what works with what you've got to compete with....in your league.* That formula helped save my businesses.

∞

I don't believe in three modern-day myths: *"Get over it.",* *"the past is the past."* and *"live in the present."* Never have and never will for three reasons:

1. The past is a motivating force.
2. Bad history doesn't repeat itself; we repeat bad history *if we aren't aware of it, don't study it, and don't change.*
3. What passed will make the present and the future.

The past is made up of good history and bad history. We're blessed with the miracle of long-term memory. I've chosen not to delete memories because, good or bad, they will teach me what to do next. So, I don't let it pass because the past has paradoxical power – it can make you or break you. It can bring you peace or break you to pieces. There's a clear line between living in the past and learning from it. Learning from the past takes deep introspection – hardcore research to ace the test, not casually looking it over with headsets blaring music at the same time. What you do with the past will shape your present and future. The past can be a crushing weight or the strength to lift it. The past can weaken you or strengthen you. It depends entirely on how you exercise freewill. You can make conscious decisions for today and tomorrow based on what you learn from yesterday or you can ignore the past and waste one of the most valuable learning opportunities that can make the difference between winning big and losing big.

I don't live in the past, but I've made a personal pact with myself to not repeat the nightmare parts that almost buried my businesses in a growing commercial graveyard of failed ventures. You can't change mistakes made in the past, but you *can* prevent them. Additionally, you can repeat past successes. You can make them happen again. It's impossible to quantify every business lesson I've learned or to list them in a neat order from number one to ten. Investigating my past keeps uncovering pieces to a growing puzzle that, although it never seems to build the perfect big picture, fits together better and better. However, just when it looks like all the pieces finally fit, a mess happens. The puzzle falls apart, more pieces are found, and the current pieces sometimes don't fit any more. Nonetheless, the key is to *stick with it* – keep studying. Build a case. Find the evidence. Mysteries are fatiguing, but they don't solve themselves. The leading cause of unsolved mysteries is giving up *right before the solution was ready to appear*. Building a business to last takes a personal vow: *give up giving in*. Eliminate the option of quitting. Erase the word *quit* from your vocabulary. *Fix it, don't leave it*. That mindset doesn't just happen. First, you have to *grow some, and show some*. That starts in your heart and soul.

∞

I believe that the starting point to self-generated business survival is figuring out whether you have the soul of an entrepreneur. The E-soul is the business owner's inner support system that has a special calling branded on it, preparing you for the demands of bringing a new business into the world and then protecting it with your life. The problem with figuring out if you have an E-soul is learning *sign-language*; learning to read signs that typically make no sense or can be taken two ways. Figuring out your calling is the equivalent of trying to decipher new-age messaging – short-forms, bad grammar, misspelling, incomplete sentences, and fragmented paragraphs. It's like trying to learn a foreign language without an instruction manual. Self-taught sign-language often turns out to be a guessing game.

My E-soul symptoms were clear and simple to read. Two symptoms kept surfacing: risk-taking, and the inability to work for anyone. A non-conformist, easily susceptible to boredom, missing the follower-gene. At first, I chose to ignore the symptoms. I convinced myself it was normal to be different, maybe even a passing phase. But the condition got worse. From what I've experienced, standard workplaces fear risk because of a one-sided focus – the focus only on the dark-side, never on the bright side. The standard focus is on the potential loss, not the potential winning. Risk doesn't stand a chance when only one potential can be seen. When the potential of consequences obscures any potential of reward, then risk changes character – its own individual character, and team character. When fear of loss conceals all potential of gain, something happens in the mind that spreads to the heart and soul. It shuts them down. Eventually, the psychological edge is lost, and then *everyone* is on edge.

Professional growth is paradoxical. It can make you or break you. The longer I stayed in one workplace, the more I craved a challenge, but it was no longer available, leading to a condition I called *out-of-control*; completely unable to work for anyone. I felt totally outside the controlled environment of limiting workplaces confined by chains-of-command. No one needed a chain-of-command more than I did as a rookie. However, professional growth breaks that chain. If it doesn't, the chain will strangle. If you're working in an anabolic workplace where you can continuously grow, stay there. Don't leave. If you're not, catabolic workplaces are hell. Workplaces that stunt your growth declare psychological war between your mind, heart, and soul. Eventually, your conscience starts taking shots…body shots and head shots until you make a choice – resign or resign. Resign yourself to a controlled life of intellectual decline until official retirement kicks in to pay you until you kick off, or resign from hell, take control of your mind, and go to the next level; all with the clock ticking. No timeouts. The call has to be made, one call after another that decides what direction you take: up or down.

I believe that psychological warfare is one strategy used by your inner support team to get your calling across when you've blocked the messenger and the message. It's a simple message, direct and to the point. It worked on me, but I was a tough one to crack. I had next-level tolerance for the pain of workplace hell. Pain-tolerance is paradoxical. It can make or break you. If you can't take what you're supposed to take, you will end up in dead last. If you take what you're not supposed to take, same place – dead last. Nothing leads to losing faster than mixing up your threshold for pain. That's why it took me so long to make the right call – crossing up the pain thresholds. The reason for my stubbornness and ignorance was the same each time – love was stolen. The thing I loved to do the most at my workplace was taken away, so my spiritual team used its deadliest weapon to accomplish its mission – assholes.

Crossing patterns are not created equal. We cross paths with those who we want and those we don't, but both are needed. They serve the same purpose. People we love and people we don't love both steer us where we are supposed to go. In my case, every career move was made after my spiritual team brought out the heavy-hitters; the big guns, workplace assholes who stole my true love. They took away my passion, the one thing that drove me to work every day that balanced out the workplace hell. My spiritual team used a next-level hell to get me moving along to the next assignment. The message was clear – if you won't go peacefully, we'll drag you out. As it turned out, use of force wasn't necessary, because having my true love taken away is the only push I needed. Having my true passion robbed couldn't be replaced at the scene of the crime. I had to go out and build a new one, or build on to my old ones by using my passion more wisely.

I believe that we're all used the same way to help others follow their call. Sometimes we're the good guy, and sometimes we're the asshole. Our assignment depends on the situation. The next call may not make sense, but we have to execute. We have to develop skills to carry out the assignment. Sometimes that calls for being nasty. Someone's got to play the bad guy for the good guy to win.

∞

Eventually, I listened to my calling, and started my businesses as a solution to workplace hell. They were an escape, but I built another hell by making one of the *worst business mistakes I ever made.* I compromised. I tried to be a part-time business owner. That didn't work, because it multiplied hell by building another layer. I learned the hard way that there is no such thing as a part-time business owner; just a deadbeat business owner who starts something and then hands it off to someone else to take care of it. As a part-time business owner, I became the equivalent of a part-time head coach; a misleader who appears by convenience, sometimes shows up for practices when convenient, sometimes shows up for games when convenient, sometimes calls the plays when convenient, sometimes picks the starting lineup when convenient, sometimes draws up a playbook when convenient, and always shows up when the team wins…but disappears when they lose. I learned that I could be fully-invested or not invested at all. There's no middle ground with investment when survival is on the line. Part-time investment is appropriate for what doesn't matter. I also learned that I could be either a head coach or a player. I couldn't be both. There's no such thing as a player-coach, just a player who can't coach, a coach who can't play, and a split-personality who can't see the truth.

The moment I made the decision to leave it all behind and become a full-time business owner, my eyes opened up to what I never saw, and could not see before, because I was getting in my own way. I was blocking my own view and blocking out the light. I stood between who I was, who I wanted to be, what my business was, and what it was not. My business was dying. It was not living the life it was intended to lead. It was unfulfilled and underachieving. It was wasting potential, draining energy, and growing old before it reached its prime. It was weak, out of shape, and getting hammered mercilessly. It was stuck in last place. The business had no pulse. It wasn't living a full life. It was just barely existing.

That's when my investigation into our losing business turned it around. I had to research my man-made business-hell to find out how to change it. That's how I found a secret of what works *in our reality*, and what doesn't work *in our reality*. This series lists the conclusions I reached, insights about how to sell H.E.L.L. in our personal, customized hell, and how to survive. Here's an introduction with the top 12 disciplines of what I've learned in our business reality:

1. *There is no straight line to self-made business success.* It's impossible to give clear concrete directions from point-zero to a strong, healthy business. There is *no generic secret formula* that is guaranteed to work in every reality. The secret is to find what works in your reality and *build a system* accordingly.

2. *Nothing just happens.* You choose to win. You choose to lose. The universe is not against you. There's no conspiracy to keep you down. You make conscious decisions that lead to first place or last place. You can play the victim or play the champ. You become who you play. Play the strongest, become the strongest. Play the weak, become weak. You choose who you play voluntarily. Choose who you play wisely.

3. *Every day in private business is a sudden death playoff game.* Someone moves on, someone is eliminated. One win is never enough to win a championship, and winning big is not enough. Staying on top is even tougher. There are no get rich quick schemes. There's a natural struggle attached

to all success by whatever definition of success you use. The struggle is painful and unavoidable. It's part of a merciless business Darwinism, a natural selection that will separate weak from strong businesses. No grievances and no union protection will defend the weak. You either get better or become extinct. Every day in private business is Game 7; someone advances, and someone goes home.

4. *A big price must be paid.* Full investment, full interest, and full return. There is no such thing as low interest, low investment, and high yield. It's pure delusion to believe that you can make your own business work with minimal investment or minimal interest. Low interest, low standing. Zero interest, zero wins.

5. *Fight your fears and don't flee from them.* Solve problems and don't run from them. Never underestimate the power of your fight/flight switch. One will make you, the other will break you. Business survival depends on which direction you move – toward or away from problems.

6. *D.U.I. is business life or death* - **D**ecisions **U**nder the **I**nfluence of fatigue determine whether your business lives or dies. A secret is working it out when you're not tired. All quitting happens when the mind convinces the body that it's over and that time is up. Don't listen to your mind when it's telling you to pack it in. It's a trick. The mind is weaker than the body. Listen to your heart and soul instead. Train harder. Beat fatigue. Stick it out. Stay in the game. Do not drop out at the first sign of pressure, stress, or fatigue. Work it out by working out. If you're unwilling to train and change weakness to strength, your business is doomed to an untimely death.

7. *Manage the clock wisely.* Clock management determines where your business ends up in the standings. Clock management is more than time-management. It's *waste management*. How *waste of potential* and *waste of time* are managed on any team is the first measurement of true leadership.

Waste management is tied to every leader's universal calling – *bring out the very best*. Bring out the *very* best in every individual and the team. Zero waste builds winners. Zero waste of time and zero waste of potential builds championship teams. *If you can't control waste, waste will control you.* Waste is a leading cause of losing streaks, and hardcore evidence of *misleadership*. A team cannot coach itself. Lead by coordinating. The *power of coordinator-leadership* is a force of nature and nurture that will build a championship on any field and in any field. A self-coached team is not a team. It's a mob. A misled crowd of people going off in different directions guided solely by self-interest.

8. *Money is not a business's primary focus. Making an impact is* the top priority. Making money is an outcome. It's a by-product of making a powerful impact. Focus on making the biggest difference, and that will make the biggest difference in your income. If you make no difference, it makes no difference what you do, because you'll make no money at it.

9. *R&R is a secret to business survival.* Customer **R**ecruitment and **R**etention is a business's true scoreboard. The rate and percentage of R&R is the number one indicator of business survival. No other evidence is more convincing or compelling. The key is the sequence – first you have to recruit and retain customers, then they have to recruit and retain your business. *Two-way R&R* is a secret to making your business win.

10. *Master the basics…then stretch.* The power of the basics is a force of nature and nurture. The way to turn a losing streak into a winning streak is to master the basics, and then stretch. The biggest cause of a losing streak is the failure to master the basics – repeated automatic second-nature execution of the fundamentals. Overlooking mastery fundamentals guarantees losing. You can't move to the next level until the basics are set. Raise the bar. Reach higher. Go to the next level…and then the next. Setting stretch goals raises levels

of consciousness, building a championship mindset faster and deeper than any other method. Setting stretch goals stretches performance.

11. *Conscientious* is one of the most important words in business. The elusive search for the number one leadership trait, employee trait, and team trait that guarantees peak performance boils down to one word: conscientiousness. The winning personality is wrapped up in that one word. Conscientiousness is not a trait; it's a *personality*. It's the number one factor that gets you to the number one spot in the standings. Conscientiousness encapsulates every single trait that you need and are looking for. A conscientiousness player will do all the things needed to win. A conscientiousness team will do all the things needed to win championships. A conscientious business is guaranteed to survive any struggle. However, conscientiousness doesn't just happen. It's built.

12. *Work will win.* Dual meaning. First, it's the championship statement: blue-collar work ethic is essential to winning in any field; business included. Secondly, it's a formula: work + will = win. Work is not created equal. How you define work determines exactly how far you go. Work is an abstract concept, open to multiple interpretations. Everyone has a personal, customized definition of what work means. If you nail the definition and live it, you will build a willpower that will never accept losing as a final score. The inescapable truth is this: out-working your competition guarantees winning, because winning is a war of will. Yours and theirs. Winning is an outcome, not a goal you write down and dream about. Winning and losing are results, by-products of the always present *cognitive dissonance*,[3] the individual

---

3   Tribute to a masterpiece, A Theory of Cognitive Dissonance (1957) by Leon Festinger. Evanston, Illinois; Row, Peterson. The theory of cognitive dissonance has profoundly influenced a number of skills and strategies I have used in my professional careers including how to get the truth from a crime suspect, how to get the very best out of an athlete, college students, and myself.

and team inner conflict that either makes you or break you. Lifts you or limits you. No person is conflict-free. No team is conflict-free. Here's the bottom line: what you do with conflict determines where you end up. Conflict is fuel. It builds one of two burners: a soul on fire, or an inner hell. Every business, every team, and every person is constantly tested with the same conflict-challenge: solve it or spread it. *Unresolved conflict* is the number one cause of all hell; failed businesses, failed relationships, crime, losing streaks, finishing dead last, underachieving, anger, rage, depression, frustration, resentment, and the calling-killer...bitterness. *Unresolved conflict* spreads like a next-gen virus. *Solved conflict* is the catalyst for all next-level performance, all winning, and all championships. Conflict is a challenge that tests what we've learned so far and what we're supposed to learn next. Solving conflict is the most important work that a coach does to build a winning team. *The biggest conflict stems from not knowing what to do. Being lost leads to darkness.* Teach what to do, and you solve the biggest mystery. Work will win.

∞

According to accounting rules, a business entity is separate and distinct from its owner...but that's on paper. Ultimately, a new business and its owner don't run along parallel universes. They intersect, mesh, and eventually morph. Business and owner are joined at the mind, heart, and soul. They share the same blood type. They spill the exact same guts. However, what defines them is their *disturbances* – cause, effect, and solution. What determines their boundaries is the full effect of *cognitive dissonance* on both the owner and business. Cognitive dissonance is the inescapable inner conflict, also known as guilt, which builds up when you act contrary to your beliefs. When we contradict ourselves by acting against our true self by doing what we shouldn't, not doing what we should, doing less when we had more to give, not doing what we're capable of, when we know we can do more but settle for less, when we sell out instead of putting out, when we give in instead of digging in, when we run from a fight, and *when we let it slide*. Guilt is not a wasted emotion if it matches the crime and *if* it becomes a change agent. Don't fear inner conflict. It's natural. Fear not having a solution. Fear running away from it. The stronger the cognitive dissonance, the stronger the fuel. *The stronger the soul on fire, the stronger the desire, the farther you reach higher...* if you make the right call. What you do with conflict decides the fate of your business and your fate as a business owner.

∞

My businesses are life-savers. Never underestimate the power of a self-generated business. Mine saved me from several layers of hell. The hell of conflict-ridden workplaces, the hell of unfulfilled potential, the hell of underachieving, the hell of boredom, the hell of an unchallenged mind, the hell of being controlled, and the worst hell of all: retirement. Being a business owner is not a retirement job. It's retirement-replacement. My businesses give me a job for life. My businesses give me a compelling purpose. Business is my sport, and I don't have to retire from it. Retired is for the tired. Tired leads to retired, retired leads to being tired.

This book series lists some of the lessons I've learned about how to start a high-risk business from scratch in high-risk places, and beating the odds by surviving in an industry that has a dreadfully low life expectancy. These are some of the lessons I've learned the hard way from *selling H.E.L.L. in hell*. I started counting at *point-zero*. The drive was erratic, and it's still in progress, but we've got a better sense of direction.

∞

Chapter 11

The basics: The power of a 6-pack.

"Those were special times, Gino, which I will never forget! Thank you for the memories!" – Lee Flores

When I was a police officer, I had to read the *"caution"* and the *"rights"* to arrested people suspected of committing heinous, unspeakable crimes. I had the equivalent of having my rights and caution read to me by lawyers, accountants, and every expert and self-professed expert you could imagine when I decided to start a business from scratch:

"I have to warn you of the high-risk you're taking. You realize that you're starting a high-risk business. Do you understand that 90% of high-risk businesses fail? Especially the high-risk business you're starting. Do you still want to start a brand new business from scratch after having been warned of the risks?"

It didn't stop when the businesses started. After my businesses kicked off, I had the last rights read when conventional thinkers thought my businesses were ready to kick off: *"Have you thought of pulling the plug?"* Outside of next-to-kin, no one encouraged. I never heard, *"Keep plugging away. Never pull the plug."* The psychology of starting a business is different than anything I've experienced because of word association – *new business = fear*. The mere thought of starting a new business strikes fear – fear of risk, fear of losing it all, and fear of hell. The overwhelming fear that *"new business"* invokes can disconnect you. In my case, I had no business mentors, no coaches, and not even cheerleaders. Starting a business is a mystery. Making it survive is a bigger mystery. Selling H.E.L.L. in hell is the biggest mystery of all. Gym and books attract sympathy. My businesses get treated like a sick relative – sad-faced. *"How's your gym doing?"* Advance condolences. That awkwardness about whether or not to avoid a depressing topic. When do you bring it up, and what exactly to say?

I've learned never to expect any meaningful dialogue about business. It's not a prime topic in social circles, professional circles, or inner circles. I've learned never to expect outside encouragement, to never depend on external motivation, and to never wait for inspiration. The most powerful motivation is deep inside you. I lift myself. What worked out for me is needing it and demanding it. When you need it badly enough, you'll demand it from yourself. *Wanting* it won't cut it. *Needing* it will force you to make self-demands that will drive you to do what others think you'll never be able to pull off.

Every job I've worked has been extremely challenging. Every career I've had has the pressure of a steep learning curve that can make you or break you. However, only one is a consistent threat to lose everything you own. The job of *business owner* has been my only career without secure, financial guarantees that paid me regardless of performance, regardless of success or failure, and regardless of winning or losing. It's the only job with a true scoreboard that publicly announces where you stand. It's the only career I've had where uncorrected mistakes will break you financially. It's the only job where you can lose everything you own, but it's also the only job where I have had psychological freedom, where I fully controlled my own mind, my own personality, my own time, my own potential, and my own destiny. That's part of the *beauty of owning your own business.*

The *beauty of owning your own business is not being forced to rely on those who don't show up.* Absentees. Those who don't show up physically or mentally for work. Absentees in body, mind, or soul. Those who give half-assed or even less effort for what they're getting paid to do. Being forced to rely on absentees builds the most confining limits. It's a restraining barrier to your personal potential and your team's potential. Absenteeism is the leading cause of losing. No team can consistently overcome absenteeism. Being forced to work with those who don't show up for work physically or mentally dooms you to a last-place team.

The *beauty of a owning your own business* is waste management; the ability to control the five deadly wastes that destroy a team and quality of individual lives: waste of time, the waste of mind, the waste of talent, the waste of work, and the waste of potential. Waste mismanagement is the number one organizational plague that I have witnessed in my almost forty years of working for other people. Waste mismanagement is the direct result of incompetent leadership – *letting it slide* intentionally or unintentionally. Letting a team waste its gifts is irrefutable evidence of coward leadership – fleeing from a problem instead of facing it and fighting through it. Letting it slide is caused by abdicating leadership responsibilities – organizational neglect that stabs at the heart and soul of a team in any field. There are three leading manifestations of waste management: hiring the wrong person, poor training, and rewarding weak performance. Waste mismanagement boils down to one problem, the single-most powerful negative force that will bring down a team and individual performance and potential: *weak conscience.* A weak conscience is the root of all waste. A weak conscience strikes at the heart of a team and each person on its roster. Left unchecked, a weak conscience will bring down any team in any field, straight to the hell of dead last.

The *beauty of owning your own business is controlling the ceiling,* the ability to control your limits – to push limits or let them push you down. Every job I've worked in had ceilings – intellectual, emotional, physical, and financial limits. Ceilings are imposed and lowered by the people who run teams. Organizational ceiling-control is governed by a set of dynamics steeped in conformity. Owning your own business puts you in control of ceiling height and weight – you can lift it or let it crush you. It all depends on how you exercise freewill, and self-generated business allows you the freedom to exercise it fully.

The *beauty of owning your own business* is the *survival challenge* that lets you test what you've really got by facing a merciless, unforgiving business Darwinism that will rip-up the weak and cut them from the lineup. The pressure of keeping a business alive is a crushing weight that either makes you or breaks you depending on *what* you can lift and *who* you can lift. Surviving selling H.E.L.L. in hell is directly connected to its lifting capacity. Selling H.E.L.L. in hell won't work out unless your business has the *soul of a lifter*, the core strength to lift customers, giving them an experience and feeling that they will want and then need again and again. The beauty of owning your own business is having the freedom to build, develop, and shape the soul of a lifter, the brandable core strength that is capable of making a seismic impact on as many lives as you can. The beauty of owning your own business is the self-control to make the biggest difference. Owning your own business gives you full control of the difference you can make.

Core strength is the backbone of lifting capacity, and an essential for business survival. A new business has to be in top-shape long *before* opening day. Don't make the mistake of waiting until you get in the game to get in top shape. Be in top shape *before* you line up because a business's rookie season is a make or break season. Business Darwinism doesn't include a grace period. Business Darwinism is a ruthless natural selection process; a force of nature that operates by the *90-10 rule:* 90% won't cut it; 10% will.

The good news is that being a 10%er will likely keep you in the game. The bad news is that being a 10%er will not guarantee winning big. It lets you win a few, and it lets you lose a few. Championship Darwinism has a different set of rules starting with the *body- temperature ratio: 98.6 - 1.4. 98.6%* won't end up in first place; only 1.4% will. First place in business starts inside the customer's mind. Moving up in the standings in the customer's mind moves you up in the league standing. If your business, or product, or service is not in the first place in the customer's mind, you'll never end up in first place overall. You'll never win big. You will never win it all. You'll never build a dynasty.

A championship business is built exactly the same way as a championship sports team. The *basics* are the same. There are different courses to negotiate in your specific reality, but the fundamentals are the same. The core of winning is universal. However, building a championship business doesn't just happen. Winning big has to go through a natural struggle. There are no short-cuts and magic formulas that randomly lead you to first place. Building it will not guarantee first place. Building it will not guarantee that people will show up – customers or staff.

At minimum, aim to be a 10%er. That starts at the grassroots level, meaning, *building the base*. The base is the foundation of *grassroots winning. Work in, work out, work up;* the three-directions of winning. One of the biggest mistakes in starting a new business is to try to raise the ceiling before the base is solid. The base is the core of a new business that will keep it standing straight up in the face of intense pressure. Grassroots training and grassroots campaigning are a secret to core strengthening, the systematic building-blocks fundamentals that form the guts of your business.

After the base is built, reach higher – raise the bar and be a 1.4%er. Getting there takes more than core strength. The business has to build overall extraordinary strength and stamina; a *power- endurance* that emerges only when all weaknesses are removed. Weaknesses in a new business are more than flaws; they're the soft spots that won't hold up to intense pressure. Soft spots are caused by half-assed training. An untrained team is an oxymoron. It's not a team. It's an imposter. A poorly-prepared, inexperienced team that is not game-ready will get annihilated. Soft spots are the direct result of misleadership, that is, amateur coaching.

Building extraordinary core strength doesn't just happen. It will not happen automatically or randomly. Extraordinary core strength, like extraordinary weakness, is the direct outcome of conscious decisions. Building a rock-solid base is the culmination of pain-staking teaching, learning, and infinite practice reps that develop hardwired second-nature performance leading to hardcore expertise. Building a base doesn't promise longevity. It doesn't guarantee staying strong. Core strength needs consistent *high-quality work investment*. Otherwise, the business gets flabby and out-of-shape, distorting its appearance and performance to a break-point where it will get sliced and shredded.

A weak, out-of-shape start-up business will never survive the hell of a fiery natural struggle that business Darwinism forces every new business to endure without fail. The key is a strength and conditioning program that builds business armour. The basics of building core strength is the *6-pack,* six fundamental power tools that will build your start-up business into fighting shape:

1. The power of growing some and showing some.
2. The power of the E-soul.
3. The power of soul-control.
4. The power of blood and guts.
5. The power of making an impact.
6. The power of the blue-collar.

∞

Lesson #1
Grow Some, Show Some

Fear is fuel.
Fear fuels F-Bombs.
Fear fuels fight or flight.
Neither one just happens.

One of the greatest obstacles to overcome in deciding to start a business from scratch and saving it from dying an early death is not the competition, it's not insufficient funds, it's not a poor location, it's not bad service, it's not designing the right logo, and it's not writing the perfect business plan. One of the greatest obstacles is overcoming fear. The fear of risk, the fear of uncertainty, the fear of going broke, the fear of full-force investment, the fear of critics, the fear of yourself, and, the most scary one, the fear of what needs to be done. Fear is a powerful F-bomb that can make you or break you, depending on which F-bomb switch it pushes: fight or flight. One will break your fear; the other lets fear break you. Which F-bomb switch is pressed depends on conditioning. Past training. Habits. Hardwiring. Programmed memory.

Overcoming fear by fighting it starts at the top: growing some and showing some; building an iron-will mindset. Growing some and showing some starts with the two basic elements of attitude toward fear: how fear is perceived, and what your past response to fear has been. These two elements are connected. The common denominator that connects them is hell. Fear is hell, and feeling fear is hell. How you perceive hell determines exactly what you'll do – escape it or run from it. Fear is either a challenge that lifts or a challenge that crushes. A blessing or a curse. You either feel the rush or rush away. Face it and fight it or turn and run as fast as you can. Each reaction becomes a *hell-rep* – one repetition toward what you'll become: a fighter or a runner. Those are the choices that determine whether you will start your own business and whether you'll keep it alive. Wanting to start your own business is not enough. Wanting it to work out is not enough. You have to make it happen by pushing the right switch.

After more than a decade of trying to make high-risk businesses work, I've learned that very little is more important than the mental strength to handle the back-breaking pressure and gut-wrenching stress of solving potentially crushing problems that, left uncorrected, will cannibalize your business and make you lose everything you own, everything you have worked for in your entire life, your sanity, your heart, and your soul.

If you want to start your own business from scratch with your own money, your own ideas, and with no strings attached, an important part of business survival is growing enough and showing enough at the *exact time* it's needed. Then, grow more and show more, and more, and more. There's no such thing as having some too big. It's impossible to have some oversized when it comes to protecting or losing everything you own. Here's the reason why: if you don't grow some and show some, you won't fight to the death to stop your business from dying. Your start-up business is guaranteed to stare right in the face of death at some point in an early age. Defending your business from dying works inside-out; starting inside the owner and bursting outward to every aspect of the business. Protecting your own business from an untimely death takes every fibre of physical, intellectual, emotional, and spiritual courage as well as strength. Without growing some and showing some, the pressure of a self-generated business becomes a crushing weight that will make you give up and give in. Your business will be doomed because of weak-will. Iron-will is a self-made business's greatest resource. Every other resource is secondary.

If you're unwilling or incapable of fighting for your business's life, don't bring it into this world. Don't start a business that you will not defend with everything you've got. Spare the business the grief of a torturous, untimely death if you don't have some or won't show some when it's time to show the most. All the business knowledge, and education, and book smarts, and titles, and experience with working in other people's business are useless if you haven't grown some or won't show some to defend your own business from daily attacks on its existence. The job description of a self-generated business owner starts with *lifeguard*. First and foremost, your job as a business owner is saving the life of the business that you brought into the world. You are in charge of security, and you're a defence administer. You are the defender who has to protect and rescue the business from an onslaught of assaults… including self-inflicted attacks.

The only guarantee in business is the continual threat on your business's life. Nothing else is guaranteed; not an income, not happiness, not reaching maturity, not even tomorrow. A self-made business will never escape assassination attempts externally and internally. Before any self-made business can grow to next-level strength and health, a base has to be built to withstand rookie-season pressure in order to save its business life over and over again during its formative years. Life-saving needs basic survival training that starts with building your commitment and self-discipline *before* building the business. Don't wait until *after*. Growing some and showing some is the fundamental part of a self-made business. No other business strategy, or tactic, or trait, or experience is more important. Timing is crucial. Make sure you grow some *before* you start a business from scratch and *after* you cut the ribbon. Waiting until the business is alive to grow some will be too late because you'll always be playing catch-up. The business will outgrow you. You can't show what you don't have. If you don't have any before your business opens, you won't be ready for the biggest fight of all – the rookie season. A business's rookie season is one of many layers of hell that needs all of what you have to escape from before it burns you up and consumes every fibre mentally and physically. What will save you during the rookie season and every season afterward is the *soul of an entrepreneur.*

Lesson #2
The Power of the E-soul:
The soul of an entrepreneur is a business owner's and business's core strength.

I believe that *nothing just happens.* Nothing happens randomly, and nothing happens automatically. We make things happen or we don't make things happens through ongoing choices of free will. I believe in synchronicity; connections instead of coincidences. One outcome is connected to another even if we don't immediately see it or understand it. What matters is what we do about it. I don't believe that DNA and nurture explains everything about what we can become, are supposed to become, and will become. I believe that there's more that shapes us than what we genetically inherit and how we're raised. I believe that our souls hand out our assignments, and push us, and drive us toward it whether we like it or not. I believe that our souls work with a spiritual SWAT team led by our guardian angel, because I don't believe that everything just happens. I don't believe that a big bang somehow landed all the working parts miraculously perfectly synchronized within the Laws of Nature inside the unimaginable limitlessness of a universe that, despite the wo/manmade chaos on Earth, is free from disorderly conduct. Everything is perfectly spaced apart; the sun never burns up planet Earth, nothing slides off planet Earth, and miracles of life repeat themselves every day on a planet that somehow manages to stay on course, never straying from its orbit.

The *soul of an entrepreneur* is not just a catchy title to brand and sell a series. It's real. The soul of an entrepreneur is the reason I started my businesses, the reason why I left at the height of two professions, the reason why I could no longer work for anyone, and the reason why I developed a dread at the mere thought of going to workplaces where mobs were lining up to get hired into what Hollywood made movies about. I believe the soul of an entrepreneur is the driving force that opens a new business and makes it survive. The E-soul makes it happen by connecting the links that form a chain-of-events leading to the birth and development of a new business. The E-soul was our business life-saver – it eventually saved our businesses from a burning hell that I managed to expertly build by ignoring it. If you're debating starting your own business, soul-searching is essential. Find out for certain if you have the soul of an entrepreneur because the E-soul is the core strength of both the business owner and the business itself.

The *soul of an entrepreneur* is a calling that never stopped pushing and pulling me in the direction of what I was supposed to become and supposed to do. The soul of an entrepreneur is a nagging voice that never remained silent. The volume kept getting louder until the message got across. When the noise didn't work, it resorted to an inner slugfest to decide whether to stay or go. Leave workplace hell, or suffer it out until old-age pension kicked in doing something for the rest of my life that I had outgrown. My soul of an entrepreneur fired an inner hell that became my driving force. It lit a fire and poured fuel on it that, depending on perspective, was punishment for ignoring my calling or a reminder to keep moving forward toward my new calling. Depending on one's point-of-view, my E-soul was a blessing or a curse that fired double-barrel guilt – guilt for not being happy with careers that others would sell their souls for, and guilty for not growing some and showing some by doing what my heart told me to do and prepared me for.

The soul of an entrepreneur can be your strongest ally or your worst enemy. It depends if you follow it or resist it. If you follow, the soul of an entrepreneur will coach you to grow some, show some, push you, and drive you to become who you're supposed to be and do what you're assigned to do. If you resist it, there's hell to pay, because a calling is non-negotiable. The E-soul doesn't ask politely, or request timidly, or suggest, or recommend, because a calling is a performance demand.

You can't beat the soul of an entrepreneur; not its calling and not its drive. It's an unstoppable force. The soul of an entrepreneur is a soul on fire. It will drive you to where you're supposed to go, and it will teach you what you need to know…the hard way. The E-soul is an inner fire that just won't go out. If you try to put it out, you'll burn up. The E-soul is an essential part of the 6-pack that builds core strength. If you're missing the soul of an entrepreneur, do not start a business. You won't be cut out…you will get cut out. Save yourself from getting cut up and cut out of the game.

Lesson #3
The Power of Soul-Control: The Fight for Freedom

It's easy to rip your soul apart. One way is guilt. Another way is to forfeit soul-control. They're connected. One leads to the other. You have to lose soul-control and then get it back to fully understand it, appreciate it, protect it, and fight for it. But once you've taken it back, your personal soul-control is one of the 6-pack basics of building core strength; a fundamental power tool that will build your start-up business into fighting shape and keep it that way.

I was taught the power of gratitude. I had it hammered into my head since childhood. I believe in the infinite power of gratitude. Gratitude adds up – it's the best way to count your blessings. However, where's the line that separates gratitude from guilt? Can you be thankful and contemptuous at the same time? When my professional growth stopped, my dislike for workplaces grew…and so did my guilt. I've been conditioned since birth to shut up and work and to be thankful for any job I've been blessed with because my parents reminded me constantly that I didn't know the true meaning of misery and depression. I was part of a spoiled generation, having been spared abject poverty, hunger, and war.

When my workplaces became hell, my conditioning kicked in. I lived with it. I resorted to what I was taught to do: shut up and work. Whining was for children. Show up for work and outwork everyone to prevent the embarrassment of being labeled lazy. Yet, eventually I bumped my head on the ceiling dropped by every one of my jobs and workplaces, starting the cycle-of-loss. The challenge had ended. My personal growth had stopped. Another call was being made…but it went unanswered, and soul-control was lost. Once the challenge was gone, everything went with it. The need to grow isn't optional. It's a call for service. It's a call for training. It's a call to prepare for the next assignment. By not answering the call, I lost soul-control to a workplace that could no longer provide growth. It was no longer part of the plan. Not only that, but I wasn't alone. Not one day went by without hearing statements-of-contempt by co-workers about their jobs and workplaces. I have a theory that when workplace challenge is gone, conflict-compensate replaces it. When there's no room to grow, inner conflict spreads to outer conflict, leading to the poisoned workplace. A dangerous mix of combustible substances blend together to build radioactivity that breaks the toxicity meter.

Darkness blocks out light. Light blocks out darkness. I believe there are dark places built out of the ravages of unresolved conflict. Policing exposed me to the depths of social hell, where hatred eclipsed any ray of light. Poisoned workplaces exposed me to another layer of social hell, where frustration, bitterness, and anger not only shut off the lights, but cut the power source completely. Dark places leave you with limited choices. Grin and bear it, join the fight, or escape.

I tried the first two choices, but they didn't work out. Both caused me to relinquish soul-control to those who were controlling my professional life. Losing soul-control is a gut-wrenching feeling; like a death in your inner circle. There's temporary relief depending on the degree of self-deception through the rationalization, the justification, and all the bullshit I threw at myself trying to convince myself of a lie: that staying in a toxic workplace was noble, honourable, responsible, and gracious. Thankfully, my conscience never stopped speaking straight from the heart. My conscience saved my soul. I re-gained control by taking the next step: becoming a full-time business owner.

Everything we do is a next step. The only thing that stops us from taking the biggest step is guilt. Guilt is what tortures the soul; the soul doesn't torture itself. Guilt is the voice that cross-examines you, trying to wear you down with fear-mongering attacks to win the non-confidence vote:

"What if you fail?"
"Why can't you be happy with what you've got?"
"It's not normal to feel this way."
"Why do you have to be different?"

The best professional decision I ever made was becoming a full-time business owner. It gave me full control of my soul just when I needed it most, and it gave my businesses what they needed most to survive. The psychology of *why* a self-generated business is born determines whether it lives or dies. Give your business a *compelling purpose* and it will give you *compelling meaning* that will fuel your fight for business survival. Compelling purpose and compelling meaning are essential 6-pack fundamentals for core strength. My businesses have a primary purpose: to give me *soul-control* and let me keep it. Compelling purpose forces me to bring out the *very* best in myself and my business team to *recruit and retain customers by making an impact on their lives.* There's no other choice. No alternative. Losing soul-control is not an option. That's why purposes are not created equal. Strength of purpose depends on level of need. How bad you need it determines how strong the purpose is. Strength of purpose determines exactly how hard you'll fight for what you're fighting for.

Soul-control is how I keep score. My scoreboard is by how much control I have over my soul. My businesses are a fight for psychological freedom that I refuse to lose, because once you've got soul-control, you will never give it up. Never. *The need for soul-control is one of my strongest business motivations.* Money, material, titles, benefits, and pension will never replace soul-control. Controlling your destiny, your potential, and your personal growth are basic survival needs. The reason I believe this is hardcore evidence is because I've *felt* the pain of having my soul controlled by workplaces, not jobs, which limited personal growth with side-show distractions that attracted continuous unresolved conflict – externally and internally. I can't stress enough that none of my jobs were soul-controllers; my workplaces were. I have been blessed to have worked in the best professions known to wo/mankind, but great jobs and great workplaces are two separate concepts.

Jobs drove me, but workplaces drove me away.

You cannot fully control your personal growth while working for someone else, because you can never fully control the resolution of conflict. The lack of control to prevent and resolve conflict is the single-most inhibiting force that limits personal growth. At the heart of soul-control is the ownership over conflict-prevention and conflict resolution. Unresolved conflict is a slayer. Unresolved conflict is the leading cause of personal and professional hell. Causing continuous conflict is a social plague. Those who are addicted to starting conflict are filling a psychological void. The drama of conflict adds meaning to an otherwise meaningless life. Unresolved conflict is the biggest waste of time that humans can endure. Broken focus turns into broken dreams, which become nightmares, that is, physical hell, intellectual hell, emotional hell, and spiritual hell. Unresolved conflict is a team-malignancy. Conflict-builders are team toxins. Those who can, do their job. Those who can't, start conflict, because starting conflict is a replacement for working. Personal soul-control is the only escape I have found from workplace conflict. Soul-control is the key to crime-prevention, the prevention of conflict that will slide your team and yourself to the hell of dead last.

I have a theory that every human has thought of being her/his own boss for at least one moment in time. The reason I believe this is because of *statements of contempt.* Conservatively, I've heard about 20,800 statements of contempt about jobs; contempt for bosses, workplaces, co-workers, being overlooked and overworked, broken promises, and no promise. That estimate doesn't include the depressing countdown to retirement, or the sad pension calculation marked by the calendar check-off where the disgruntled and disillusioned wish away significant chunks of their lives waiting for their official release from hell. End of a sentence. Parole. That number would make a decent Facebook following, a sold-out arena, or the population of a small city. A controlled soul is not a happy soul.

Compelling purpose is not isolated to one's self; it's connected to the world by the need to present the *very* best product and service, to make the biggest impact, to make the biggest difference, to make an indelible mark, and to do something that won't be forgotten. Fighting to keep soul-control breaks limits, turns ordinary into extraordinary, and lifts any heavy weight that's put in your way. To fully appreciate the power of soul-control, I first had to lose it. I underestimated the full-force of soul-control without a point-of-reference. The process of losing soul-control and winning it back raises your level of consciousness, building a heightened awareness to what matters most in life, what needs to be fought for, and what needs the full-force of all your heart and soul.

We obsess over hair, teeth, clothes, muscles, fat, wrinkles, and every body part that flames the fire of inner hell, but we easily ignore the most important and vital part of us: the soul. Get a regular soul check-up. X-ray your soul. Clean up any dark spots before it's too late. If you are trying to decide whether to start a business from scratch, or trying to decide whether your current business is really worth fighting for, shape up by reminding yourself of what life was like when you forfeited soul-control. There are plenty of soul-lifting programs that can help, but they all take some blood and guts.

Lesson #4
The Power of Blood and Guts:
Change Your Perspective, Change the Outcome

You will fight for what you spill your blood and guts for.
You will give up what you don't spill your blood and guts for.

The first step in building a new business's core strength is *transplanting* and *transparency*. The moment you make the decision to start a new business from scratch is also when you have to transplant your heart and soul into your business. Not only that, but your blood and guts have to be clearly visible to everyone – to the public, your team, and to you. Here's why:

- The heart and soul are magnetic forces; they pull people into your cause. Speaking from the heart and acting from the soul attracts a powerful following. Movements don't just happen; they're inspired.

- Blood and guts make your business real. True authenticity. A clear public view of your business's blood and guts removes any mystery. Visible blood and guts guarantees the highest credibility rating. Disingenuousness detracts; genuine attracts.

- Seeing your own blood and guts is a reminder to fight like hell for what shares your blood and guts.
- Putting your heart into your business gives it a pulse.
- Putting your soul into your business gives it life.
- Putting your heart and soul makes your business indispensable.
- Spilling your blood and guts into your business will save your business from losing its blood and guts.

The survival mindset and the will to stay alive depend entirely on the *dispensability factor.* Dispensability determines what you fight for and what you will give up. What is dispensable won't be fought for. Only what is indispensable will be defended from death to the death. Indispensability switches on the greatest inner force: the fight switch, the self-generated performance demand that accepts no alternative other than surviving. No other choices, no escape, and no running away. Indispensability triggers the primary psychology of business survival: *need it, demand it.* If you truly need your business, you will demand it stays alive. If you don't, it won't. Need is not created equal. Ordinary need won't cut it. You have to need it like your next breath. The only need that will stop you from losing your business and everything you own is the top-of-the-line need: *basic survival need.*

A dispensable business is at risk. The truest high-risk business is the heartless, gutless business; an empty business that is not desperately needed. Without full heart-soul-blood-guts investment, any business is a high-risk business. The greatest threat to your business isn't a sinking economy or skyrocketing gas prices, it's a lack of undying, unconditional commitment to your business's survival. The biggest risk is a lack of demand and supply; no demand from your heart and soul means no supply from you blood and guts.

I learned about the *power of perspective* the hard way. I started my businesses without the right perspective of what the business truly represented – a business that you start from scratch is your *wo/manmade soulmate.* That perspective makes your business indispensable. It makes you naturally and automatically spill your blood and guts to defend it, protect it, make it grow, and bring out its very best. Don't start a business from scratch if you will not spill your guts to defend it from dying. Don't start a business if you don't see it for what it truly is: your *wo/manmade soulmate*. If you don't see your new business as your *wo/manmade soulmate*, your business is dispensable. You will leave it in the hands of someone else to take care of...or leave it altogether. If you don't view your business as being your heart and soul, killing the business will always be an option when the fight gets too bloody. You will fall to the temptation of pulling the plug when they're flipping the pages to find the last rites.

Changing your perspective will change the outcome. Change the way you view your business. When you see your business as your heartbeat and your pulse, you will change the outcome immediately.

If you're going to back out, you will back down.
If you're going to back down, don't get in.
If you're going to get in, invest fully.
If you won't invest fully, you will pack it in instead of backing it up.

Lesson #5
The Power of Making an Impact is Pain-Relief

If you want someone to stick with you no matter what, *make an impact on them!*
If you want someone to back you up, *make an impact on them!*
If you want someone to go down a dark alley with you, *make an impact on them!*
If you want your team to go undefeated, *make an impact on them!*
If you want to fill the seats, *make an impact on them!*
If you want perfect attendance, *make an impact on them!*
If you want to pack in an audience with standing room only, *make an impact on them!*
If you want them to join up, *make an impact on them!*
If you want them to keep coming back for more, *make an impact on them!*
If you want them to remember you, *make an impact on them!*
If you want them to spread the word about you, *make an impact on them!*

Make people feel important, and you'll be a star attraction.
Making people feel meaningful makes you the main attraction.
Making people feel different positions you in first place…
…But giving them a *sacred memory* makes them never forget you.

Core strength is measured by the consistency and outreach of impacts that a business makes. Making an impact is the difference between a dead business and a live business. There's a direct relationship between the impact-consistency, size of impact, and business longevity. A business lives for as long as it makes an impact. If it stops, so does its pulse. The force and frequency of impacts makes or breaks a business. First place goes to the fittest – the biggest impact-maker.

An impact has two main elements:
1. Contact – two or more people have to cross paths.
2. Change – a difference has to be made.

Business survival depends on crossing paths with customers repeatedly. When contact is made, a repeat of crossing paths will re-occur only if a positive difference is made. The customer's situation has to improve. The customer's problem has to get solved. The customer's life must get better. A business is a change agent. It has to be willing and capable of effecting change each time a customer crosses its path. Consistency of change is a secret to customer retention. The expectation and realization of a positive change will make them come back.

When there's a meeting of two or more, an impact always happens. A change is guaranteed.[4] Whether the impact is positive or negative depends on intent. Motive determines impact, and vice-versa. The cycle repeats itself. Impacts change motives; motives changes impact. Meeting people can lift us or limit us. The outcome depends on strength of motive. When the intent to effect positive change overrides all limitations, an impact will happen.

4   Tribute to a masterpiece, Locard's Exchange Theory. My business theory of impacts has been adapted from forensic scientist Edmond Locard's 1927 theory that contact between two causes a traceable exchange of substance.

There in lies a key to building core business strength: the intent to overcome obstacles to produce positive change.

Wanting to make an impact is a universal basic survival need. It's one of the most powerful motivators because of what it does – pain-relief. Relieving someone's pain relieves yours. Relief brings relief. Pain-relieving is a powerful, addictive feeling – having it relieved and making it relieved. The inner reward of relieving someone's pain is unmatched...so is the inner reward of beating pain. Both are victories. Both are big wins. Customers will never buy H.E.L.L. in hell unless H.E.L.L. relieves more pain than it causes... and the customer is aware of it. Pain-relief is not always obvious and not always apparent. Often, it has to be pointed out. Selling H.E.L.L. in hell depends on instruction such as teaching customers the pain-relieving qualities of H.E.L.L., proving it, and *ensuring they know it when it happens.*

An impact is the elusive feeling that humans continuously search for in the never-ending quest to escape two of the many killers of happiness: boredom and underachieving. Monotony of daily life and not reaching full potential are two of the top-rated life pains that trigger the furious chase for a cure. Boredom and underachieving are connected, working together to fuel the inner hell of being stuck in the rut. When we find a solution, we're hooked for life. Stimulation sells. Pain-relievers are addictive and impactful. Pain-relief is the impact we're all pursuing. Pain-relief is a secret to business success. A business that relieves pain will survive and live a long prosperous life. Pain-relieving is the business anti-aging secret. Take away pain, and you will get rich quick; emotionally for sure, and maybe even financially. There is no greater inner reward than relieving someone's pain. Being a pain-reliever is a gift, the greatest talent that you can be blessed with. If you are a proven pain-reliever, commercialize it, because then you're in business. The power of making an impact is a business's core strength – an unstoppable force of nature and nurture, as well as a soul of a business on fire.

However, there's a fine line between pain-relieving and pain-inducing. Pain-relieving talent doesn't just happen. It's built over time. Along the way, we can cause as much pain as we take away…sometimes more. People are forgiven. Businesses are not. When a business causes more pain than it takes away, the business is unforgiven.[5]

Selling H.E.L.L. in hell depends on making seismic impacts. Ordinary impacts have a shelf life. Impacts are not created equal. There's strong and weak impacts; positive and negative impacts. An impact is an impression made on the mind, heart, and soul. Impressions are not created equal. Some are temporary, and others are permanent. It depends on the force of impact – speed, size, and the actual point-of-impact. Impacts are eye-openers or eye-popping, head-scratchers or head-clearers, but each one is a life-changer that sets a course, and one step in another direction. Every impact sets a course brought on by conscious decisions we make and don't make. Selling H.E.L.L. in hell will fail unless H.E.L.L. keeps the customer on a direction straight out of hell.

There is no greater impact than the *sacred memory*, the thriller that can't be put into words. Sacred memories are like a big win, the miracle comeback, the turnaround, doing what was believed impossible, David thumping Goliath, the beyond-wildest-dream coming true. Sacred memories are the true secret to recruiting retention and recruiting, because sacred memories travel faster than the speed of sound. They have the strongest magnetic force. Sacred memories are awarded a V.I.P. position in current and potential customer's minds. Sacred memories are not subject to the ruthless memory Darwinism that ravages the storage of filed information. The human memory has an unforgiving natural selection process that can drop your business from first place to last place in the blink of an eye. Survival of the fittest memories means the strongest memories stick while weak memories get deleted.

A secret to making sacred memory is goose-bumps. The more you lift them up, the bigger the impact. The bigger the impact, the stronger the memory. The stronger the memory, the more often your business gets visited. High-impact businesses are naturally selected. Low-impact business won't survive the cut.

---

5   Tribute to a masterpiece, The Unforgiven. By Metallica.

Lesson #6
The Power of Blue-Collar: Tipping the Balance of Power

If you can't take it, it'll break you.
If you do take it, it'll break you.

The paradox of what you take and what you don't depends on the extent of core strength from point zero, the moment you get the idea of starting a business long before your business actually opens for business. Core strength is not created equal. Selling H.E.L.L. in hell needs heavyweight strength, that is, *blue-collar core strength*. Starting a business without blue-collar core strength exposes a weakling to the high-pressure, high-stakes world of the big-leagues. A soft, weak new business will get crushed. First, it will end up in last, and then it will be dismantled piece-by-piece until it drops out of the competition.

A business trying to survive is exactly the same as a sports team trying to win. Winning is the objective in sports. Winning is *first place*. Winning is championships. Winning is conventionally quantified by scoring more points against your competition. However, winning often gets confused with a final score, two numbers side-by-side that tell the conclusion but not the full story. Winning is much more than what is lit up on a scoreboard. Winning is the *big picture* – the context. Winning is the sum of every single fibre, physically and mentally, doing its job to its *very* best, first behind the scenes and then on the stage. Winning is a by-product of spilled guts and stains – sweat stains, dirt stains, and blood stains. Winning doesn't just happen. Winning doesn't happen simply by showing up, by luck, by accident, or by entitlement. Winning is the end result of a Darwinian process that pummels the weak into the ground, tearing apart 98.6% of those who line up. Winning is a natural selection process that rewards and awards the survivor of a struggle that will bust up the unprepared and uncommitted. Winning is an ideology in motion; a practical application of systematic beliefs. There are no short-cuts to winning. True winning will never allow the by-passing of a struggle that does one of two things: crush the weak or transform the weak. The natural struggle makes you choose – break down or break through. Winning is not a participation sport, it's a survival contest that measures what you've grown and what you've shown. True winning is serious business in real-life because real-life losing costs more than politely handshaking with your competitor and going for ice cream. The true scoreboard of winning and losing publicly displays whether you have grown some and shown some at the moment of truth *when it counts;* whether you are getting better or getting worse, and whether you're moving in the right direction or not. Athletics teaches every single lesson needed to win in business. The sport's model won't fail in business if it's followed to a T. Winning in sports also depends on blue-collar core strength. Winning and losing in any field is directly tied to blue-collar core strength.

All winning starts at the top with *actus vocare* (call to action) and *mens opus* (work-minded). Together they form the *blue-collar mindset.* The difference between those who do and those who don't is willingness and capacity to form a *compelling intention* to make it happen. Warm, fuzzy positive thoughts and upbeat dialogue won't cut it. Thinking about it and talking about it are not enough. All that matters is doing it. Getting it done takes a special kind of thinking, a compelling intention, a powerful motive that will find an opportunity to get it done. If no opportunity is found, a compelling intention makes its own opportunity happen. Compelling intention doesn't just happen. It's called out by an inner force: *actus vocare,* the inner call to action. *Actus vocare* is more than positive thinking, more than fluffy inspiration, and more than feel-good motivation. It's a driving unstoppable force that won't quit, won't give in, and won't give up. The drive is fueled by the *mens opus*, a work-mindedness that turns thought into performance. *Mens opus* is single-minded purpose that converts intention to doing *until it's done.*

Actus vocare calls it out – calls out the inner beast and calls out the outer beast. Actus vocare calls out your *very* best to compete against the *very* best. Mens opus puts it into motion. Together they form the blue-collar mindset that gets it done no matter what. The blue-collar mindset wins in any field – sports, business, public sector, wherever performance has to be called out to fight for first place.

The psychology of the blue-collar mindset stems from the *dual pain-threshold – zero-tolerance* for suffering the pain of losing, *high-tolerance* to break the pain of struggle. The difference between first place and dead last is the *blue-collar pain threshold* – what you tolerate and what you don't. Where you end up in the standings, in any field, is a measurement of how much you take and how much you won't or can't

Zero-tolerance is premised on rejection – non-acceptance of last place and all the unstudied losing and uncorrected failure that leads to it. It's impossible to build a winner of any kind without *zero-tolerance* for the unacceptable. Zero tolerance for a half-assed job, for getting embarrassed, for letting down the team, for not backing up your teammates, for ignoring what coaches teach, for not showing up for work physically and mentally, for ripping-off customers, for ripping-off employers, for being gutless in the face of intense pressure, for amateurism, for immaturity, for being selfish, for being spoiled, for being soft, for not spilling your guts for the team, and for not giving your very best. Zero tolerance for punk behaviour. Zero-tolerance for the pain of incompetence, ineptitude, apathy, and lethargy is essential for winning it all. *If you take it, it'll break you.*

A high-tolerance for discomfort is needed to break through struggles instead of breaking down. A high threshold for pain is essential to keep working when you feel you can't take it anymore and when you think you have nothing left to give. Winning happens when you can take it after your competition can't take it anymore. Whoever can give more when you can't take any more, wins. *If you can't take it, it'll break you.* A low-tolerance for pain and suffering will simply cause more. Those who can't take it, never make it.

You make what you take. What you make happen depends on what you are willing or unwilling to take, capable or incapable of taking. You can't confuse what you take. You can't mix it up. You have to take what your competition can't, and refuse to take what others will. Leadership has been written about and talked about as much as any topic in the history of wo/mankind. Leadership boils down to building the proper pain-thresholds and not mixing them up. Build up the right tolerance; don't build up the wrong one.

Tolerance for pain is the product of conscious decisions. Don't complain about what you tolerate and what you don't. If you can't tolerate the pressure and stress of hard work, don't blame bad luck, bad circumstances, or bad people. Blame yourself. Get better. If you tolerate laziness and incompetence, don't play the victim and don't ask for martyr pity. Don't look for sympathy. Look in the mirror at the problem and fix it.

Build up your tolerance for work. If you suffer from work-aversion, don't start a business. If your collar isn't blue, put on a white collar and work for someone else. Lower your tolerance for team toxicity. Habitual high-tolerance for half-assed work is a sure-fire sign to stay away from starting a business. A high tolerance for mediocrity softens the underbelly of a self-made business. Lower your tolerance to zero to build your business's core strength. If you're unwilling or incapable of adopting a zero-tolerance policy for losing and last-place finishes, you will become your business's greatest risk, its most dangerous threat, and its worst nightmare.

Nothing has stronger building-power, more staying-power, and more magnetic-power than a blue-collar team. A blue-collar guarantees building a winner from the inside out. A blue-collar builds upper-level core strength that won't crumble under everyday pressure. It'll withstand the worst and work through the rest to become the best. Blue-collar power is a secret to the *upset;* the miracle win that no one expected.

Every new business's survival is an upset because every new business starts as an *underdog.* Underdogs have attraction power. People relate to underdogs because there are far more Davids than Goliaths. People root for the underdog who will out-work natural talent – yours and your competitors. Working past your own natural gifts and working beyond your competitions' natural gifts always makes a compelling story. David versus Goliath fights never get stale. There's no such thing as too many sequels, because *stains* are appealing and attractive. Sweat-stains, dirt-stains, and blood stains always draw a crowd because they yield high-interest. A Goliath knockout by David is a sacred memory that guarantees the spreading of word-of-mouth through the ages. No story spreads faster or farther than a win for the blue collar underdog, because the blue-collar team does what everyone hopes to do: *tip the balance of power.*

A small percentage of the strongest start-up businesses cut it and end up in first place. An overwhelming majority of the weakest businesses get cut or end up in dead last. The difference between first place and last place is the power of the blue-collar, the tireless workwo/manlike mindset that is guaranteed to work through any problem, fight through any pressure, and overcome any adversity that gets in the way of your livelihood. The power of a blue-collar is in the *reps* – sustained workload through repeated exertion of effort. *Reps* are a secret to shifting the balance of a business's power from abject weakness into upper-level core strength.

Weakness is not created equal. Weakness is relative. Weak means *not as strong as the fit* that survive the natural struggle of a brutal, unforgiving natural selection. Without exception, every new business has a natural struggle that it must pass through. There are no detours and no shortcuts. Contrary to popular myth, there are no get-rich-quick schemes. There are no overnight successes because of the *infinite reps rule* – it takes *infinite reps* to become good at something, eventually becoming better than 98.6% of your competition. Becoming a 10%er is almost good enough...for second or third place. However, to lock up first place, shoot for the 1.4% group. The 98.6% line is the success threshold that guarantees winning at anything you try to achieve. *If you do it better than 98.6% of your competition, you will keep cutting it. You will never get cut.* The good news is that becoming a 1.4%er guarantees business survival. The bad news is that it will not happen in one day, one week, one month, or even one year in most cases. Infinite reps take a long time. Infinite reps are the heart and soul of the blue-collar mindset, but they take blood and guts to get there.

The reason why the majority of rookie businesses fail is *not being ready to play*. Not being ready to play happens when *weaknesses outnumber strengths* needed to compete at the level of competition you're trying to survive in. The imbalance of power rule is a main reason for business failure – limited strengths with unlimited weaknesses. When weaknesses outweigh strengths, you have an inner-power shortage that tilts the playing field against you, meaning you don't have enough power to cut it at your competitive level. The imbalance of power is the weakest starting point for a new business, making it frail, fragile, immobile, and unable to move forward and cope with the viscous pressure of its rookie season. Trying to cut it at the next level is a monumental challenge, because it calls for the building of strengths that didn't previously exist and beyond what can be imagined. You have to go places you've never been or even thought of. To be ready to play, a new business has to be in top shape, a shape that hasn't been experienced. A new business can't wait until after the game starts to get in shape. Born weak, stay weak. That's what happens when weak choices are made. A weak rookie business has no hope of surviving the cut. The only solution is blue-collar training *before* the real season starts, building core strength before opening day.

Turning weakness to strength is an agonizing change process. Growing pains always hurt. That's the leading cause of rookie business's mortality – the agony of growing pains stops the full extent of the next-level preparation needed to win big. Pain is prohibitive. The unwillingness and incapacity to endure pain is the reason why rookie businesses are born weak, stay weak, and die. Upping your pain-tolerance is vital for business survival. Raising your pain threshold is crucial to build your business's strength and get in contest shape so your business won't crumble and shatter the first time it gets hit. If your business can't take a hit, it will get knocked down, stay down, and cost you your financial life. Crossing higher and higher thresholds of pain is not an option, or bonus, or fringe benefit; it's a basic survival need. It's impossible to survive in business with a low tolerance for work-induced pain. Unmanaged hurt is the leading cause of shutting down a business before its time.

A weak start-up business will invest all its energy in trying to stop the bleeding. It's impossible to build core strength needed to survive business Darwinism while constantly trying to recover from getting beaten and bloodied. *You can't heal and get to the next-level at the same time.* You have two choices when you decide to open a business: suffer the pain of training *before* the game starts, or suffer the pain of dying *after*. The difference is whether you tip the balance of power. The solution is tapping into the power of the blue-collar.

∞

Chapter 12
The E-soul: look inside and call it out.

The concept of *perfect timing* is a matter of perspective. How did I know the perfect time to start a business? When it was time to escape hell. How did I know the perfect time to become a full-time business owner? To escape another layer of hell. However, I didn't see it at first. I had to change my focus, my vision, and my language. I had to change my perspective, but that takes time. You have to invest time to effect any change. The most valuable investment I made into my business was conducting an investigation; a self-investigation to find evidence of the soul of an entrepreneur. I needed to go deep and solve the mystery. Did I have the essential E-soul to survive in a self-made business? I had to look inside and call out to my next calling. Here's what happened: I discovered a trail of evidence, did some forensic testing, and the results poured in on time. They were deadly accurate – 100% positive. But it took me a while to understand the results. I didn't get it at first. It got me.

When it happened, I re-defined "perfect time", and found a synonym: hell. They have exactly the same two components – challenge and control. When my jobs lost their challenge, hell started. When my personal growth became controlled and stalled by strangers who had the title of manager and administrator printed on their public sector calling cards, those personal ID hand-outs conventionally and mistakenly called "business" cards, another layer of hell formed. Loss of challenge and loss of control over my personal growth simultaneously became hell, and the perfect time to escape it by becoming a full-time business owner was staring me straight in the face…Except I was too busy to stop and tell time.

The perfect time doesn't have the convenience of a traditional alarm clock. You have to read the signs to figure out the perfect time…and that takes time. Investing time to investigate yourself, read signs, translate omens, interpret messages, and to *take the call* is a process. It takes time and investment to answer the call. However, I was preoccupied with fighting. As it turned out, I was fighting no one, fighting nothing, and fighting for no true cause. I was fighting with my eyes shut and my heart closed. I conjured up a movement that stuck me in a place that I had outgrown. In retrospect, I had tried to create meaning of what had become meaningless. I was compensating for one of the great confusions of life: lost passion for what *used* to be a passion. I refused to accept that my emotional attachment to my careers had been severed. I couldn't admit the truth: I stopped loving my jobs because organizations came between us. I no longer loved what I used to love with a passion, because loss of challenge and loss of personal growth leads to the biggest loss of all: loss of stimulation. My jobs became easy, predictable, and repetitive – the three signs of personal apocalypse, the three signs of boredom, and the three signs of mind-numbing monotony. It's one of the top two ways to torture a soul…the other is guilt. Both lead to the same place: unresolved conflict, that is, hell.

Unresolved conflict is the cause of every single problem in the history of wo/mankind. It's the cause of all hell. It's the cause of all crime, every war, all battles, and all breakups. Then there are the real ones outside your mind. Internally and externally, unresolved conflict brings out our very worst. Unresolved conflict is the leading cause of losing. Unresolved conflict is the main reason for ending up in dead last. The difference between winning and losing in any field and on any field is how conflict is managed or mismanaged. Conflict mismanagement is the difference between last place and first place. The secret to all leadership and all frontline performance is what results from conflict. Is the conflict converted to fuel that drives you and your team, or fuel that burns you up? The paradox of conflict can make you or break you.

The paradox of conflict is also connected to the *perfect time*. It creates it. Unresolved conflict is an environmental hazard. There's no greater waste of time and energy than unresolved conflict. Unresolved conflict is a clock-killer, team-killer, and even a potential killer. Unresolved conflict removes discretion, making the decision to leave and start your own business easier – a virtual no-brainer…if you can recognize it. In my case, I couldn't pick it out of a line-up at first. To my defence, my perfect time was culture shock. I have never expected to have the soul of an entrepreneur.

Take a close look at your conflict, past and present. There's a message there if you study it close enough. Investigate your conflict expertly and you'll find secrets as well as solutions. Take your time. Don't rush. Don't overlook any piece of evidence. No sign is too small or too insignificant. Don't look past the past for relevance. Don't make impulsive judgments about what seems to be irrelevant. The past is not to be dropped, or dwelled on, or lived in, but it has to be investigated to prevent the same old crimes. History doesn't repeat itself, we repeat history. Build a case for your future by piecing together hardcore evidence, not just speculation and baseless opinions. Big pictures are built one concrete piece at a time.

Be careful of mismanaging conflict. Be careful managing workplace conflict and inner conflict. Use extreme caution with how you manage hell. Mismanaging hell is the leading cause of losing streaks, the linear path of habitual failure that leads to more and more layers of hell. Hell is not a mystery; it's paradoxical. Hell will make you stronger and tougher than the rest[6] if you fight it and escape it. Getting the hell out is the path to first place. Expertly managed hell builds winners. Beating hell wins championship rings. However, if you fight it and stay in hell, you will get burned out and burned up, becoming a weakened mess that needs awakening. Mismanaged hell is the worst distraction that won't just break your focus; it'll shatter it, cutting it to pieces. It doesn't just side-track; it derails.

Never take hell lightly. Long-term battles with hell get you nowhere. Finish it. Throw some bombs. Burn 'em deep. Don't get into a prolonged ground game. Find the quickest way out and save your soul as fast as you can. Don't let hell make a comeback. Take your perfect time to escaping hell. Don't wait for it to happen on its own. If you're trying to decide whether to start a business from scratch, dig up the evidence, find out if you have the soul of an entrepreneur, and make the call. Decide. Make your E-moment. Open your eyes. See what's in your soul, and your heart will tell you what to do.

---

6   Tribute to a masterpiece, Tougher than the Rest. By Bruce Springsteen. A must for all lifting iPODs.

If I had waited for the conventional perfect time, when everything seemingly falls into place, I never would have started any business, and never would have become a full-time business owner. I'd still be controlled and unchallenged. The conventional perfect time is utopia, the risk-free, pain-free fictional place covered in pink bubbles, unicorns, and rainbows. There is no such place where nothing can go wrong and nothing can hurt you. Such a conventional perfect time and perfect place will never happen. You have to make your perfect time happen. The perfect time won't happen on its own. You have to build it, starting from the inside. The perfect time to make any change is when you've had enough and when you decide not to take it anymore. Turnarounds happen when you lose your tolerance for where you're at. It takes conscious decisions, one call after another. You will get to first place when you decide not to take last place anymore. You'll start winning when you decide not to take losing. Only when you can't take hell will you escape it. If you accept hell, you'll stay there.

Freewill has a strict exercise plan – escape hell and avoid hell. Decisions are hell-oriented. They're an escape plan or a prevention strategy. Choices are made to get out of an existing hell or prevent going to one. Freeing oneself from outer hell frees the soul from inner hell. The perfect time to start a business is when you need to save your soul. Here's one sign of the perfect time to start a business: if you have a soul on fire and there's no room to fly, no room to move, and no room to break out. If your soul is burning to takeoff, but there's no place for liftoff, it will burn you up to a crisp beyond recognition and beyond the salvage point. Working for others has tremendous benefits – literally and figuratively. If your job strengthens your soul, keep it. If your workplace pumps up your soul, stay there. However, if your soul is burning in a hell, it's a perfect time to revert to an exercise plan.

The perfect time is when your E-soul is on fire.

∞

Chapter 13
It's an offense to pass or run from your calling.

I firmly believe that a calling is a series of answered calls, dropped calls, and calls put on hold. I believe we have a calling stamped somewhere on our soul made up of one assignment after another, after another. The assignments all have the exact same objective: make an impact. Assignments may have different job descriptions, but there's no difference in the end result of making an impact. It reminds me of an unconventional defensive football position, called the X-Man, I created in our system to solve some of our annual roster problems. Instead of just one job, the X-man has to re-invent himself and constantly evolve to do several assignments. Sometimes he's a linebacker, or a defensive lineman, or a defensive back. Rookies ask, *"What am I? What's my job? What do I tell people?"* Impact-maker. Tell them you're an impact-maker. It doesn't matter where you line-up, it doesn't matter what direction you have to take, your job is exactly the same as everyone else's job on every play: make an impact. Make the biggest impact possible again, and again, and again. When you stop making an impact, you've resigned. You just cut yourself.

I believe you can't pass on or run from your calling. I believe that callings are not optional. They're performance demands. We have the freewill to follow or reject our calling, but choosing "no" isn't accepted by the soul. It doesn't take rejection lightly. I believe that we're led along the way to make our calling happen in the form of signs, messages, omens, and synchronicity. When we don't understand our calling, or flat-out decline, there are consequences to help us; push, us, re-direct us, to give us a second chance to think it over. The consequences range from mild grumpiness to a burning inner hell.

I believe entrepreneurship is a calling. It's a vocation. It's a compulsion deep down in your soul that draws you to what you're supposed to be and what you're supposed to do. *Vocation* is derived from the Latin word *"vocare"*, which means *to call or voice from God.* That's why I believe calls for service are serious business, why calls have to be answered, and why dropping calls or putting calls on hold just won't work out and won't cut it. Callings make us fit in...just like building a football team. If I gave players complete autonomy to fill the roster by letting them choose their own positions and the starting lineup, there would be chaos; pure unadulterated hell. Deep-rooted conflict would kill the team, never letting it get off the ground, because everyone would fight for the spotlight positions – quarterback, running back, linebacker. No one would sign up for the grunt-work, those blue-collar jobs in the trenches that let the stars shine in the spotlight. When players are assigned their position, trained for it, given the full-force of coaching-attention, told why their position is vital for the team, and then see the importance of their assignment, then, and only then, do they understand the true impact they are having on the big picture; namely the success of the team, not just success of the individual. The same can be said for the starting lineup. Starting jobs are not handed out like treats to win popularity contests. They're earned for the benefit of the player and the team to eliminate the greatest threat of all – being unprepared and unfit for the viscous savagery of the game. There are two types of cruel and unusual punishment:

1. Letting a starter rot on the bench as a second-stringer.
2. Letting an unfit second-stringer start.

Both will suffer badly for being out of place. I believe the same happens with our calling. Our vocation is a never-ending work-in-progress. We really don't get to choose our position, but we do get to choose how we perform. We choose what we do with our training. We choose if we become an all-star at our position or get cut.

I don't believe that entrepreneurship just happens. I don't believe that starting a business from scratch happens randomly, out of the blue, and for no reason. A lot of things have to happen that leads to a business opening from scratch. An alignment of circumstances has to take place, a string of plays; some that worked and some that flopped miserably. After I realized this phenomena, after I opened my eyes to the path that was being cut, I understood that I truly had no choice but to start brand new businesses. When

I raised my level of awareness by uncluttering the muddled picture I chose to stare at every day, I saw that my E-soul made a performance demand. The choice was a no-brainer. I needed to start a new business. I believe in the power of the E-soul because nature and nurture don't explain why I felt the urge to risk everything to compete in high-risk businesses without any prior warning.

I believe that a calling is an evolution. It's alive as long as you're alive. A calling is built one piece at a time by how we answer the daily and even minute-by-minute calls for service. Sometimes a call for service sends a clear unequivocal message. Other times, it sends a convoluted mess that we have to figure out. Our calling tests our investigative skills, where we struggle to find evidence to make sense out of seemingly nonsensical events that mystify our lives as we try to find our way and figure out what to do next. Our calling tests our ability to make tough calls under fire. We have three choices when a call for service is made: answer it, drop it, or put it on hold. When we do the right thing and answer a call for service, we don't need to be told we did the right thing. We feel it. First, there's the euphoric adrenaline rush, nature's free and legal pain-reliever. Secondly, there's the escape from inner hell, the inner peace harmonized by a silent conscience that rewards us with a negative… by not torturing our soul.

When we drop the call or put it on hold, we hear about it. The inner voice makes it loud and clear that we've gone off track and are heading in the wrong direction. When we drop the ball by making absurd what-was-s/he-thinking calls, or let time run out without making any call, it's easy to dismiss our illogic or procrastination under the heading of "its-meant-to-be". However, a bad play is not meant to stay uncorrected. Losing isn't punishment. Failure isn't retribution. Winning isn't a reward. They're all training. Study them. Each one needs to be investigated to discover the evidence that made the outcome happen, and to uncover what worked and what didn't. Discovering evidence leads to identifying your calling. Vocational mystery gets solved only by investigating the entire body of evidence, not by grieving losses or wildly celebrating wins.

My entrepreneurial calling didn't take a direct path. There was no straight line, no solid line, and very often, no clear line. I heard no call, saw no evidence, and never felt any passion, desire, or even curiosity for self-employment...until I fell into hell. I worked for 40 years in jobs that I loved passionately, and in places that I eventually hated passionately. That's how I finally heard my entrepreneurial calling; through the pain of an inner hell that intensely debated the professional paradox – my love-hate relationship with work. Here's my theory of how it works: I believe that the soul of an entrepreneur leads with fire; it lights the soul on fire to drive us toward what we're supposed to be, and builds an inner fire to drive us crazy when we move away from it. When jobs are firing on all cylinders, the soul lights on fire to learn the wonders of the world through *vocational experience,* learning to coexist with those who share planet Earth with us through the calling-of-the-moment, by executing the daily assignment branded on our soul. Vocational experience lets us see and feel the miracle of *reciprocal* impact; impacts made on us and impacts we make on others. Therein lies the meaning or meaninglessness of jobs – the capacity to make an impact. Does the job have a soul or not? A job with a soul enlightens and brightens. A job with no soul is an abyss; an empty hole that lets you free-fall into a limitless pit.[7]

Depending on one's perspective, a job is either a gigantic pain in the ass, or a way to experience the magic of impacts – giving and receiving them. Combined with our personal lives, jobs are opportunities to grow through the miracle of impacts. The greatest gift we receive is an impact made on us and an impact we make on others. It's a tie. We need impacts made on us so we can reciprocate and make them on others and then experience the greatest reward of all: putting up ladders for others to climb. I believe that we're all given the gift of life to maximize it – to reach our full potential, stretch as far as we can, and leave nothing in the tank. I don't believe we have the discretion to squander life and to waste it by trashing our opportunities. I believe that humanity is the big team that we're

---

7   Tribute to a mega-masterpiece, Psalm 40. "I waited patiently for the Lord, He turned to me and heard my cry. He lifted me out of the slimy pit, out of the mud and mire; He set my feet on a rock, and gave me a firm place to stand."

all a part of, and none of us has the right to ride the coattails of the superstars, hoping to win glory by loafing and watching our teammates carry the team. None of us has the right to fuck around and expect to share in our team's big wins.

If you have ever thought of starting your own business, or if you've thought of killing your business, invest some time to investigate the calls for service you answered, dropped, and put on hold to discover whether you have the E-soul. I believe self-discovery is a key starting point in making the decision to start a business from scratch or the decision to save your business's life. If you find the soul of an entrepreneur inside you, and if you listen carefully, you will hear the performance demand that will help you make the right call.

∞

Chapter 14
Finding the spark finds your E-soul.

I believe that the E-soul is the key to deciding whether to start a business or not. The E-soul connects to the parts you need to bring a business to life and keep it alive. No E-soul, no parts. I firmly believe that the leading cause of pulling the plug on a business prematurely is the empty E-soul. Either the soul of an entrepreneur was never inside to begin with, or it went missing. It was a wrong call or a lost call. My advice is simple: do not start a business without the soul of an entrepreneur. Make sure your calling is aligned with the calls you make and don't make. If you have any inclination to start a new business, invest in an investigation. Investigate your past. Start with a spark. To investigate whether you have an E-soul or not, find the earliest sign of a burning passion, and trace it back to its spark.

Until I needed to do an intensive soul-search to decide whether to leave behind my guaranteed paycheck, my benefits, my titles, and the comfort of having-it-made to start a business from scratch and become a full-time business owner, I had considered my childhood to be bizarre. I had been an obese, dysfunctional child void of social skills, feeling like a foreigner just like my parents who had arrived on a boat. Never felt in place, always feeling out of place, never learning how to be. However, if you change the perspective, you change the outcome. Taking a second look with a different perspective, I found the first evidence of an entrepreneurial soul. At the age of 12, I developed a life-long passion for working out as a solution to escape the hell of childhood obesity and dysfunctionalism. Lifting heavy weight lit my soul on fire. Or, a soul on fire lit my passion to lift heavy weight. The gym became an escape from hell, a prevention from ever returning, and the place that lets you be.

Instead of using a dysfunctional childhood as a crutch, I re-calibrated and saw its purpose – I needed to experience being a lost cause, needed to learn how to beat big odds, had to feel the struggle of overcoming adversity, and had to learn when there is hell to pay and how to make payment. I needed to feel being a lost cause because, as it turned out, I dedicated my life to coaching them and teaching them. My calling became lifting lost causes. You can't lead lost causes unless you've been one. The soul of a lifter has to go through hell first. It's impossible to discover and truly understand the secret of transforming lost causes unless you've experienced it and felt it deep inside your guts. I learned the secret by living it. Lost causes carry an inner torch, a raging soul on fire motivated by the deep need to escape hell and never return. All they need is an opportunity. Just give them a chance.

No human pushed me to the gym. No human taught me to lift. No human lit the fire. A lot of synchronistic moments had to mesh to build a life-long passion for the only sport that you don't have to retire from – working out. The spark was the hell of childhood obesity, a training ground for opening one of the highest-risk businesses – a gym. Childhood dysfunctionalism and obesity had a compelling purpose: they built the most powerful motivator known to wo/mankind, and that is the fear of hell. It develops the most powerful motivating force on Earth, and that is the need to escape hell and never return. Needs are not created equal. Eventually, that need grows to its strongest, highest level; a basic survival need. Working out to avoid a return to the hell of fat became tied with breathing for first-place on the survival-needs chart. When you need something to survive, you will demand it from yourself – guaranteed. No choice, no option, no alternative, and no escape. That was my spark. That is what lit my E-soul.

∞

Chapter 15
Soul on fire, workplace hell:
Two signs of the fire-fighter.

You need to become a fire-fighter to survive in a self-made business – fight fire with fire. To beat the hell out of selling H.E.L.L. in hell, you need a raging fire deep in your soul as well as the fear of returning to workplace hell. That's been, and continues to be, my motivation. Fire-based motivation; build a fire inside and you have fire-prevention outside. I *need* a fire deep inside to sell H.E.L.L., and I *need* to never go back to workplace hell. Ever.

Before you concern yourself with business plans, marketing strategies, sales tactics, logo colour, website design, and what title to put under your name on business cards, invest the time to do a thorough self-inventory and figure out if you have what it takes to endure the reality of a self-generated business. Understand the crushing pressure, stress, and anxiety of no guaranteed income, no tenured protection that promises a steady stream of money and benefits whether you work hard or whether you're a complete fuck-up. Understand the line-up of disappointments and setbacks that threaten everything you own. Find out if you have what it takes to resist the temptation to pull the plug at the first peek of hell. Find out if you have some and will show some each and every time when your business is under attack, bleeding profusely, and needs you to muster the courage, strength, and energy to fight for its life instead of running away and leaving it to die. It starts with the entrepreneurial soul and spirit. That's what will make you grow some. If you haven't got enough, don't start your own business, because the romantic notion of being self-employed is not enough to fight off the temptation to kill your business prematurely with self-inflicted death. If you decide to start a business from scratch, you have to eliminate killing it as an option. You have to make a pact between yourself and your business, a binding promise that you will keep it alive no matter what, that you will find a way to stay alive, and that you won't give in to self-inflicted wounds through inexperience, incompetence, or ineptitude. Having what it takes starts with the two signs of entrepreneurial soul and spirit – the fire-fighter.

If you're trying to figure out whether you have the soul of an entrepreneur, check the temperature – inside and outside. A sure-fire way to recognize if you have the entrepreneurial soul and spirit is if you're boiling inside and if it's boiling outside. A *soul on fire* plus *workplace hell?* That was the sure-fire formula that solved my personal E-soul mystery. That formula built a strong enough case that convinced me. It was overwhelming evidence that proved beyond reasonable doubt I had the E-soul, had to be my own boss, had reached a point where I could no longer work for anyone now or ever again, and that I could never return to having my professional life, potential, and destiny controlled by complete strangers absorbed in their self-interest, inexperience, incompetence, or ineptitude.

If you have an inner drive that borders on, or has crossed the border into obsession for your work, you've got strong reason to suspect you have an E-soul. If you feel that your soul is burning up in a workplace hell, you'll know beyond all doubt that you have the soul of an entrepreneur. That formula worked out for me by opening my eyes, my heart, and my soul to see what I refused to see for many years. It showed me the two immutable signs of the entrepreneurial soul and spirit. It proved that my next calling would not stop calling.

∞

Chapter 16
The power of H.E.L.L. lights the fire or burns you up.

Let's play word association:

- Working out…Pain.
- Football …Pain.
- Textbooks…Pain.

Now, imagine playing charades:

- Do a lifting motion with your arms…Hell.
- Hold two palms open simulating reading a textbook…Hell.
- Get in a three-point stance pretending to be at football practice…Hell.

My businesses sell H.E.L.L.: **H**eavy **E**xtreme **L**aborious **L**ifting; physically and mentally. If you Google "H.E.L.L. synonym", only one word appears: pain. Fitness, textbooks, football – pain. Gyms, reading, and practice – pain in the neck. Working out physically and mentally – pain in the ass.

Be careful of romance. Romantic thoughts are subjective, not objective. I used to romanticize the notion of starting my own business and selling three passions of mine – fitness, reading, and football. All three have infinite transformative powers. Each one dramatically changed my life. I *love* each one. True love. Deep love. The romance of being self-employed and making a living at what I loved to do was sexy and appealing…until I tried to sell it. I failed to understand that beauty is truly in the eye of the beholder. Just because I love H.E.L.L. doesn't mean the rest of the world automatically will. In fact, 90% of the world hates H.E.L.L. They hate the pain of working out, the pain of reading textbooks, and the pain of going to practice every day, getting covered in dirt, sweat, and blood stains. The thought of being physically and intellectually fit is appealing, but paying to do it is not.

The decision of what to sell is your biggest business decision; bigger than your sparkling new website, the fashionable staff clothes, your state-of-the-art logo, the latest secret marketing strategy, the newest revolutionary sales tactic, and your trendiest leadership style. If what you sell has no power, your business will be powerless. It will die an untimely death.

I never truly examined H.E.L.L. until after I decided to sell it. I saw H.E.L.L. as my escape from workplace hell. Freedom, soul-control, independence. I knew that H.E.L.L. wasn't for everybody, but I wasn't aware of the hell of trying to sell it. I either chose H.E.L.L. or H.E.L.L. chose me. Either way, there was no choice. I had to sell H.E.L.L. My experience led to the exactly the same place: H.E.L.L. My soul was in H.E.L.L. My only expertise was H.E.L.L. Even if H.E.L.L. was a high-risk, at least I would be selling straight from the heart. When the time came to make a decision, the call was a no-brainer: sell H.E.L.L. or stay in workplace hell. Selling it was less painful than working in it. The power of H.E.L.L. prevailed. I knew the power of H.E.L.L., but selling it meant having to convince 90% of the world it was worth the cost.

∞

Chapter 17
The 90-10 winning ratio.

If you decide to sell H.E.L.L., feel it first before you try to sell it. That way you'll understand the true challenge of your business – recruiting and retention, attracting and keeping customers in a place. That itself is a ruthless Darwinian process, that is, one that chews up and cuts up the weak. Don't expect other people to accept an invitation to stay in H.E.L.L. if you can't handle it yourself.

Find out for sure first. Before you decide to sell any kind of H.E.L.L., investigate your past and find evidence that you have experienced what you're going to sell so you can brand it with your own heart and soul. *Experience-based branding* is a key to building solid long-term relationships with customers when you're trying to convince them to be willing to pay for H.E.L.L. They need to know your story, your personal narrative, and your experience in H.E.L.L. They need to see your heart, soul, and guts spilled all over your business. They need you to share their pain. Make yourself authentic, genuine, and most of all, original. Show them you've lived it. Find out exactly why your H.E.L.L. is hard to sell. See the dark side and the bright side so you can make your pitch. It's all part of the brand that will influence a customer's decision to pay you for H.E.L.L. or not.

One reason why my H.E.L.L. is hell to sell is *work isolation.* It's made up of two concepts – exertion and seclusion. A solitary actor within a team. Isolated work-reps that add up to a team's winning or losing. Working on a team *alone*, connected through your work. Repetitive work away from the spotlight, trying to score some points to get your team the lead. In my case, working out obsessively at age 12 started a pattern that I didn't put together until I needed to make my decision to become a full-time business owner – manual labour, policing, coaching football, teaching, and writing…they all shared exactly the same DNA – physical and mental exertion in a playing field away from civilization. Never underestimate the challenge and difficulty of isolated work-reps, physically or mentally. The common perception of any isolated work-reps activity makes it unattractive. Unless there's a fire inside, isolated work-reps will drive people away at a 90-10 ratio.

If you decide on selling H.E.L.L., remember the paradox of H.E.L.L. – there's a dark side but there's a bright side. There's a powerful, life-changing, top-to-bottom transformational bright side *if you stick it out.* Consistency is the key to H.E.L.L. There's built-in motivation and potential for repeat customers if they see the light and focus on the bright side. The problem with the bright side is that the dark works like hell to overshadow it. The pendulum swings back and forth, covering up and exposing the bright side. A key to surviving in business is to *control the pendulum* – never let it get stuck covering the bright side, and never let it swing at high-speed. Eventually, break the swing, forcing the pendulum to get stuck on the dark side so that it covers up the darkness and lets only the light shine through.

My decision to sell H.E.L.L. was based on familiarity – I knew H.E.L.L. well. I knew its character, its soul, its temptations, its appeal, and its repulsion that drives people away with a high-speed getaway plan. A problem was that I knew only how to attract and keep the 10%ers, but I had no plan to convert the 90%ers. The absence of a plan, the *winging-it,* trying to convert the 90%ers, would turn out to be business hell. Before you decide on what to sell, investigate your past thoroughly for clues about what sold you on H.E.L.L. so you can plan what to sell, how to sell it, and most importantly, *how not to sell it.*

Big wins need extraordinary *private* performance. The difference between ordinary and extraordinary is the quality and quantity of reps invested *in private.* Natural talent alone is not the difference. What matters is what you do with your natural talent *in private.* Extraordinary game day reps for public consumption are simply a manifestation of *private* practice reps. How you play depends on what you pay. The cost of winning big *in public* is extraordinary reps *in private* – simulated reps that incrementally increase in challenge. Winning big is the product of training big at a 90-10 ratio for every game – 90% of winning big happens *privately*; 10% happens *publicly*. What you do privately will show publicly and vice-versa. What you do publicly shows exactly what you did privately. This rule applies to business as well. The way your business performs publicly reveals how it trained privately.

You can't bank extraordinary reps. Every big win needs a 90-10 investment ratio – 90% investment of extraordinary private reps to get one extraordinary game. Then repeat. Relying on banked past reps will drain the account. As the ratio dips closer to 50 - 50, the chances of losing more than you win dramatically increase. Banked reps are always a factor and will have some diminished strength, thus, without replenishing the rep-account with more and more quality deposits, you may squeeze out some close wins, but eventually you will start losing until you hit rock-bottom and lose big. Losing big is the product of the 90-10 rule reversed; a 10-90 ratio will get your team clobbered. When your team loses 50 - 0, your game-day reps were as lopsided as the score. 90% of your reps were game reps, but the total preparation investment was only 10% of the total reps. In this case, your opponent followed the 90-10 rule. Whoever gets closer to 90-10, wins. The bottom line is this: consistent quality training keeps you winning. Erratic, sporadic training gets erratic, sporadic performances. One-time training won't cut it. Training is a continuous *need* and a basic survival need. Training is not a would-be-nice-to-have recommended practice. I learned the hard way that the 90-10 rule applies to business. There's a direct relationship between training, performance, survival, extinction, winning big, and losing it all.

I transplanted my professional DNA to my new businesses. I decided to sell what I was trained to do even though it is one of the toughest sells. Isolated work-reps *in private* were part of my brand, so I naturally made it my business's brand. However, I made the mistake of assuming that 90%ers would buy into the philosophy that H.E.L.L. was actually good for you. True sustained isolated work-reps in private looks like hell. Just the thought scares some people. Many others are scared away in the early stages, packing it in when the exertion and seclusion confirmed what they thought – isolated work-reps *in private* are hell. The very nature of *in private* work-reps disconnects you from your social network – your real one or your artificial one. Repeated, prolonged physical and mental exertion in your own world takes you away from the friendly confines of your social network – real or fictional. Having coached and taught thousands of wannabe cops, wannabe football players, and wannabe strong wo/men, I reached the conclusion that isolated work-reps *in private* separates the 10%ers from the rest, but gutting out consistent *private work-reps* doesn't just happen. There has to be fire burning inside. That's one of the true long-term motivators that will outlast your competition – the *need* for something more than the ordinary that the soul on fire generates. You can't motivate anyone to stick around in the hell of isolated private work-reps for a long time. You can only appeal to their conscience. That's the spark and the fuel that keeps the fire alive to continuously enter H.E.L.L. Without having experienced and felt H.E.L.L. deep in the core of my guts, I never would have started a business. I would still be in workplace hell, killing the clock, counting down to old-age pension to start a life of bitter regrets. If I hadn't experienced H.E.L.L., I would have committed business suicide and homicide; I would have pulled the plug on my businesses the moment the heat turned up, when it seemed impossible to beat the odd by converting some of the 90%ers.

∞

Chapter 18
The psychology of H.E.L.L.

The decision of what to sell will make or break you. It's the difference between getting rich quick, building a financial empire, struggling to make ends meet, starving, and losing every dollar you've earned in your life.

Whatever you choose to sell, study its psychology *before* you open, *before* you make a final decision to become self-employed, *before* you quit your job, *before* you walk away from your guaranteed income, and *before* you make any other business-related decisions.

I studied the psychology of H.E.L.L. *after* my businesses opened, and *after* hell made an appearance. There's no perfect way to study the psychology of what you intend to sell. However, here's how I did it and what I learned: Working-out physically or intellectually without an audience, without fanfare, connected only to a small playing field distanced far away from the comforts of the social network, is paradoxically limiting or uplifting. Our relationship with our social network has a catch-22 effect. The paradox of social networks is the mystery that challenges all of our growth and potential. On the bright side, we all need a *true* social network for our true inner self to bust out of its narcissistic cage. We need a *true* social network to re-direct the spotlight from burning a hole in our soul. We need a true social network to see past our character-restrictive self-interests that lead to emotional vacancies, psychological emptiness brought on by self-absorption that ends in the very isolation that is dreaded by many. Having an artificial social network doesn't solve the pain of isolation; it promotes it. A *true* social network brings out your *very* best by shifting the focus from narcissistic, juvenile self-centeredness, to the soul-satisfying world of altruistic outside-interests. Putting up ladders for other is the single-greatest reward we can experience.

Coaching, mentoring, and pushing and pulling others to their next-level is an anabolic agent of personal growth – theirs and yours. Therein lays the power of the *true* social network; the extent to which it brings out your *very* best. Yet, there's a flip-side to a social network. There's a dark-side. When the need for connection to *any* social network, real or fictional, interferes with what must be done – what *needs* to be done – then the force of social networking makes you powerless. Power outage through disconnection; disconnected from your true social network by connection to an artificial, unproductive social network that occupies time and energy needed to properly invest in what has to be done to make happen what you want to happen. An obsessive need to be socially connected is a diversion from reality, a distraction from the focus needed to succeed at what you're aiming at. The unwillingness or incapacity to break away from any social network connection, especially at the expense of the work, practice, and training that needs to be done to reach your potential, is the leading cause of a growing pain called underachieving. Underachieving is a condition that leads to an epic inner hell, that is, the bitterness of not becoming what you were intended to be. Your calling won't stop calling.

Striking the balance to solve the social network paradox needs the answer to one simple question: *are you willing to do what no one else is willing to do?* Can you outwork your competition? Not just in quantifiable hours, not just by putting in time, not by just working longer for the sake of working longer. Are you willing to endure the natural struggle needed to get ready and to get in top shape? Are you willing to separate from the rest? That's the operative question that determines business survival – 13 words that separate a thriving H.E.L.L. business from one that burns in hell. How that question is answered by potential customers is the determining factor that decides your standing – first place or dead last.

The business of H.E.L.L. depends on customer and staff perception. Building your team of customers and employees depends on how they view working in private. Working in isolation is one of the leading causes of dissatisfaction and quitting. Isolation is psychologically painful. Disconnection brings discomfort. Working in seclusion tests your will, your desire, and your conscience because it's easy to fuck around when no one's looking. Change the perspective and you change the outcome. Isolated reps aren't hell if you believe it *separates you from the rest*. This is a dual-meaning perspective that changes the way you look at separating from the rest – it builds a blue-collar work ethic without the need of prolonged rest, and it drives you out of congested traffic, separating you from the 90% jammed together bumper-to-bumper, idling motionless and going nowhere. Isolated reps are a type of hell that you have to experience to make it happen. Getting what you want and where you want to go doesn't just happen. Serious off-stage training and work sets the stage. What you do without an audience determines what you do in front of one. Isolated reps prepared me for my business career by making me experience what I wanted to sell. I needed to understand what H.E.L.L. felt like before I could spread the word and convince others of its transformative benefits. You can't sell H.E.L.L. without feeling it first. You have to feel *their* pain before you can relieve it.

The psychology of H.E.L.L. boils down to need. Do you need it? Do you demand it? If customers need H.E.L.L., they will demand it. If they don't, they won't.

∞

Chapter 19
Business motivation works inside-out.

While deciding to start a business from scratch, thoroughly investigate your past for your *true* motivation. Do an honest evaluation to find out the direction of your motivation. If it isn't inside-out, don't go into business. If you have relied solely on outside motivation your whole life, you won't cut it in self-employment. Guaranteed. Why? Because no one will do it for you after you become a business owner. Being self-employed also means being self-motivated. No one will motivate you. The moment you become self-employed, you will be cut off from external dependencies, including outside motivation. If you cannot find motivation deep inside, you will go broke. Before you make any business decision, identify your strongest motivation; find the force that will push you when you feel the urge to call in sick, to dog it, to coast, to ride coattails, to watch others do your work, or to not give a shit because you feel slighted.

My strongest motivation has always been, and continues to be, an overwhelming fear of wasting my life; a fear of being bored to death, of leading a forgettable life, of irrelevance, of insignificance, and of feeling and making zero impact. My motivation is the dread of watching life fly by, of watching others live the biggest lives possible while I sit idly, confounded by the paralyzing fears that bombard us from the moment the clock starts ticking. My motivation is the potential inner hell of pissing away what I've been blessed with, day after repetitive day, stuck in a dull, soul-numbing rut without any jolt of thrill or hope of rush.

My motivation is to prevent living a life-by-default, letting the same day automatically happen, going along with what happens instead of making it happen, accepting loss after crushing defeat and doing absolutely nothing to change it, or not getting in the game at all and letting others win by default. My motivation is an intense fear of the switch shut off for good, left with dried-out adrenaline glands, deactivated T-blasts, inner cobwebs, rust, rigor mortis, post-mortem lividity, and decomposition while you're still legally alive.

My fear of living a dead life built a 24-7-365 motor that revs at high RPMs; just like my gym. No 9-5 shut-off switch; just like my gym. I never have and never will understand Monday-Friday, weekends off, retire, and expire; just like my gym. I have one goal: make the biggest impacts that stretch the farthest over and over and over. I want to make repeated impacts. I am not a workaholic; I'm a lifeaholic. Conservatively, I've been asked about 36,000 times for the secret to winning at something. I've given the same answer. Reps. Turn on your motor. Flip your switch. Ignite your high-rep, high rev. engine. I don't do infomercials selling get-rich-quick-business secrets while basking on a beach. I didn't start businesses to work less and make more. I deal in my reality which is selling H.E.L.L. in hell. I stay away from delusion because delusion leads to one place: the pain of heartbreak. What you do in your business is your business. If you want to work less and get more, God bless you. I wish you luck. I don't preach; I teach. I have no desire to ever shut off the motor. If you find the secret to make more by doing less, I still won't change. Work is not a four-letter word to me. Motivation is personal. Inner drive is customized. That's a key to business survival. Study your past, search your soul closely, and find out if you have felt the type of self-motivation that will keep your business alive. You need a scorching-hot soul on fire. Here's how I studied my past:

I've been blessed to work in six sacred professions that let me experience the power of a soul on fire; from others and from inside myself. Each career did its job – they transformed. They changed brutally limiting weaknesses into strengths. Three were paying jobs, three weren't, but they all made me rich where it counted most – deep inside. Each one was the spark and the fuel that flamed the inner fire. My careers connected me to the right mentors at the right time. I don't believe in coincidences, only connections. Every career was an intersection that let me cross paths with souls of lifters who taught me the same lesson over and over – we are put in each other's' paths to make an impact. What we do with that impact is up to us. How we exercise freewill determines the full extent and full effect of the impact. We can waste the opportunity or maximize it. I believe we cross paths for a purpose – conference calls, mutually-beneficial calling development where we build each other up and lift each other to fulfill our respective callings. It's up to us to decide whether we listen to the call and fulfill the purpose. Each impact we receive, and each one we make, is both the product of a soul on fire and the fuel that makes it burn stronger. Our relationships with other people reveal our inner body temperature, exposing whether we're boiling hot or ice-cold, whether we have a power source or power outage, and whether we charge up or drain each other. I learned the true meaning of a meaningful job – if you can truly say, *"Man, I was on fire today!"* your job did its job; it made you rich inside. If your job empties the tank and re-fills it to a new and improved upgrade, you are blessed with a purposeful job. A vocation. You're in place.

However, I also learned that if your job becomes a workplace hell that leaves you with a cold, empty pit inside your guts, be prepared to fight a bigger conflict than the one that's causing the workplace hell – guilt. The guilt of not being happy for having a job that feeds your family versus the guilt of giving up on moving forward to your next assignment. The guilt of resigning by not resigning – resigning to workplace hell instead of resigning from it. Ingratitude versus underachieving. There's a fine line between complaining about the blessing of employment and expressing the truth of workplaces steeped in conflict that will kill your soul. I worked in two public sector professions where I got paid the same for working like a dog or fucking the dog. I got the same money every week. Socialist salaries. Performance didn't matter. First place and last place got paid the same. There were no standings and no true scoreboards. Level CBA-protected playing field. Unionized security. Diametrically-opposed to and polar-opposite of entrepreneurialism. It's the worst training for an E-soul, but I needed to experience it to learn how to go broke – to learn how not to run a private self-made make-it-or-break-it business. One of the most popular clichés I heard repeatedly in both public sector jobs was, *"If this were a private business, it'd go broke."* They would. If public sector adopted pay-per-performance ideology, there wouldn't be enough to field a team – few would sign-up, and few would cut it. Guaranteed income is equally distributed to both the motivated and unmotivated.

My other careers struck the balance. My student job during high school in the grimy pit of private sector factory work taught me the unforgiving, natural selection, real-life world of 90-10 blue-collar Darwinism. If you did not shut up and lift 1,200 flour bags during every eight hour shift, you were cut immediately by getting fired or by quitting – for self-protection and the protection of the rest of the crew. No union protection, no grievance, no appeal, and no second-chance.

Coaching football taught extreme accountability by means of a public zero-sum scoreboard that calculates your competence and neatly divides up winners and losers.

Working out is a brutally accurate lie-detector test, exposing every weakness and every strength with laser precision.

Writing is the equivalent of putting your x-rays and ultra-sounds on public display, letting the world peek into your heart, soul, and guts so they can dissect, judge, and rate whether you actually have any and where they stand. There's nowhere to hide, nowhere to run, and nowhere to escape. There are no guarantees except the promise of struggle.

Each profession discussed above is a performance-based profession where all that matters is evidence; hardcore proof based on what you do or don't do. When the onus is on you to prove you can cut it, the main source of motivation that will push you past all the break-points is inside you. I found that the strongest inner motivation is the fear of embarrassment. Avoiding the pain of getting cut is an extraordinary drive because it's a manifestation of personal accountability and personal responsibility. Fear of embarrass-ment shows a low threshold of tolerance for self-incompetence. It shows you have the most powerful motivational switch known to wo/mankind: a strong conscience, and a conscience that responds to appeals.

If you are dependent on external motivation, your business career will be cut short with self-inflicted wounds. Outside motivation is a temporary solution; it's not built to last, and it won't build you or your business to last. External motivation has a small tank that empties quickly. External motivation doesn't have an industrial-sized fuel tank, and it doesn't fill up with high-grade fuel. The best you get with external motivation is the cheap stuff that will clog your motor, causing it to sputter and give out.

It's important to define external motivation and not confuse it with *external connections.* External motivation means exclusive reliance on someone else's drive and inner fire *while your fire is out.* If your fire is gone, someone else's fire will drive you a short distance, but don't expect long-distance travel. However, your inner fire is *connected* externally. It's fueled externally. People on the outside, and their causes, light your inner fire.[8] Here's my best example: a team of lost causes. When I focus on pushing lost causes to the next-level to prove the critics wrong, to show the next team of lost causes evidence that it can be done, I'm on fire. When I'm connected to their cause, nothing stops me, nothing gets in my way, and nothing is insurmountable. I don't need any pep talks. I don't need to search Youtube for motivation videos. I don't need to read Facebook for motivational quotes. *The team's cause is my cause –* that's the single-most powerful motivation I have ever experienced. When your cause is my cause, my soul boils. I will never give up until the job is done and until every lost cause finds their direction. However, when I focus on my coaching career, my self-interest, my frustration, my happiness, my sadness, my gratification, my grief, my reputation, my success, and my failure…I become an asshole. When I shift the spotlight from my players' individual successes to my own, the light goes out, and darkness sets in. What you focus on grows. What you pay attention to builds up – it either pays off, or there's hell to pay.

Exactly the same applies to a self-made business. Be careful where you shine the spotlight.

∞

---

8   Tribute to a masterpiece, Light My Fire. By Jim Morrison and the Doors. A timeless classic, a driving force guaranteed to motivate exertion.

Chapter 20
Not calling your own plays? You're playing someone else's game.

I believe that making the final decision to start a business needs a *compelling purpose*; a confluence of motives that will make you spill your guts for your business naturally, without hesitation, without prompting, and without giving it a second thought or any thought at all. You need a checklist of reasons that will let you keep score. The more reasons you have, the stronger the purpose. The stronger the purpose, the less chance you'll run and hide when it's time to fight.

Before you start a business, figure out the exact reasons why you're doing it so you can keep score. The reasons become the shared *compelling purpose* that will drive you and your business. Purpose is your business's fuel. Without purpose, your business will drain to empty, leaving you with zero desire to re-fuel. Purposes are not created equal. Some are stronger, some are weaker. A compelling purpose is the heavyweight, the strongest purpose that will refuse to accept failure. Refuse-to-lose makes for a catchy t-shirt, bumper sticker, and Facebook post. Refuse-to-lose provides entertainment and short-term bursts of inspiration during pep talks, company seminars, and motivational videos. But refuse-to-lose are three empty, meaningless words without a compelling purpose that will turn the motor which will stop you from losing your business and everything you own.

Of course, the primary objective of a business is to make money, but I believe that generating income is a by-product of a higher purpose, one greater than simply creating a job for yourself. If I wanted a job, I would have stayed in the one that I couldn't wait to leave. My compelling purpose started with the deep need to make a bigger impact and difference than I was making. Difference-making is subjective; a matter of perception. What used to look like a difference led to asking *"What's the difference?"* daily, hourly, even moment-by-moment. I had to make a bigger impact than I was allowed to. Working for someone else has a difference-making ceiling. There's a limit to what you can accomplish when someone else is calling the plays. My need to call my own plays became linked to difference-making, which connected money-making to survive independently. The *chains of control* mean you're not calling your own plays; you're playing someone else's game. That chain of control can strangle you. If you are calling your own plays, you're playing your own game. That chain of control can free you or strangle you.

I started my businesses to save my soul. That was my primary compelling purpose. I needed to stop tormenting my soul of an entrepreneur by working for other people. It was an issue of control. There's a monumental difference between being a control freak who achieves self-gratification from controlling the lives, potential, and destinies of others for the singular purpose of feeling important, and needing control of your soul's calling *after you've earned the right.* Soul-control became important to me in 1985, exactly ten years into my police career. The power of the *Decade Rule*[9] showed its stuff, and it played a big part in understanding my path to entrepreneurship, hammering home the importance of making a *calling-call*…a decision about what direction to take; to follow or reject my calling.

The Decade Rule will make a big impact on your career and your pursuit of happiness. The Decade Rule theorizes that it takes a decade to become an *expert*, a state that becomes a blessing or a curse, depending on what you do with your expertise. If you have a challenge that matches your expertise, you'll be happy, and you'll grow and move to the next level of consciousness and achievement. However, if you don't have a challenge that matches your expertise, you will suffer the pain of monotony. You will be bored to death, and you will experience the gut-wrenching agony of underachieving, which leads to bitterness, and being perpetually pissed-off at yourself and others.

---

9   Tribute to a masterpiece, The Decade Rule of Expertise. By Dr. Anders Ericsson, co-editor of The Cambridge Handbook of Expertise and Expert Performance, a volume released in 2006 (Ericsson et al. 2006). The Decade Rule theorizes that it take 10-years of dedicated practice to become an expert in any field.

Research led by Dr. Anders Ericsson showed what it takes to become an expert. The good news is that we all have hope to become an expert in our field. No one is born with expertise. Expertise is built over time; a decade to be exact. We are all given a supply of gifts and talents. What we do with them determines whether or not we become an expert at what we want to do. Expertise is available to everyone who has the willpower to fully invest themselves into consistently stretching past the barriers that stop 90%ers. Nature loads the bar, and nurture lifts it. However, there's bad news...

The bad news is that expertise doesn't just happen. Mailing it in for 10 years won't automatically make you an expert. Expertise is not a collective bargaining perk. Just showing up for a decade isn't enough. Going through the motions for 10 years will not give you the title. Expertise is not a gold watch awarded for simply raising your hand and shouting, *"Present!"* Expertise needs next-level practice – extraordinary reps. Repeated practical application of your job at incremental higher-levels of challenge. Doing exactly the same thing with no extra challenge won't be enough to earn the expert title. Putting in time, kills time; it won't build expertise.

There's more bad news – there's no clear-cut way of knowing when you've reached the expertise. The decade mark is the best-case scenario. It kicks in when all the conditions are met. When the quantity and quality of challenges actually were faced, endured, and experienced. The objectivity of what is a challenge and what is not makes the line between expert and non-expert blurry. There's no clear line of demarcation that you can simply cross. There's no scoreboard. So, how do you recognize it? How do you know for sure? When you can see what most others can't, do what most others can't and you can't put into words why or how. Making the complicated look simple is a sure-fire sign of expertise. Solving more problems than you create is another sign. When you make all-star enough times. When you reach super-star status.

However, there's more bad news: we aren't very good at self-evaluation. We humans have a tendency to underestimate or overestimate our skills and abilities, leaning more toward overrating.[10] We can be way off the mark about what we are and are not capable of. We may not be the best judge of ourselves. We may even be a mystery to ourselves, creating a fictional character inside our own minds. So we need help to prove who we are and whether or not we've earned the title of expert. We need evidence. Investigate yourself and find credible evidence to build a case. Look at your past performance. Evaluate your track record. Check the wins and losses columns. Add some witness statements from true experts who know what they're talking about, who have their own track record. And most of all, we need evidence that what we've done has made an impact on others. Whose lives have we made better other than our own? Who have we improved? What's our light-darkness ratio that we've spread around ourselves?

There's even more bad news to the Decade Rule: you may develop a strong desire for soul-control, an intense urge to call your own plays, to call the shots that affect your growth, your potential, your destiny, and your life. After a certain point in your career, after you've paid your dues and earned the right, there's a natural desire to call your own plays. The operative words are *"paid your dues and earned the right"*. You have gained enough practical experience where you have proved the capacity and willingness to make the tough calls. But, too soon is too dangerous. The freedom to call your own plays takes time; real practical experience under the guidance of a coach who will teach, correct, push you past limits, and pull out every ounce of potential that's buried deep inside. The power of mentor-protégé training is essential in building and earning autonomy. Why is calling your own plays important? Calling your own plays brings forth challenge, accomplishment, meaning, purpose, and growth. It calls forth the chain of next-level consciousness and motivation. Once you become very good at something, you need leeway to put your veteran leadership to practice. Otherwise, you stop growing, start regretting, turn sour, and become bitter.

---

10   Tribute to a masterpiece, "Flawed Self-Evaluation: Implications for Health, Education, and the Workplace," by researchers David Dunning (Cornell), Chip Heath (Stanford), and Jerry M. Suls (University of Iowa) .Published in the December 2004 issue of Psychological Science in the Public Interest, a journal of the American Psychological Society. This study provides evidence that we don't fully know what we're talking about when it comes to evaluating ourselves.

Every profession I've worked in taught me the value of calling your own plays after you've earned the right by paying costly dues. Coaching football taught me the best lesson. Rookie quarterbacks can't call their own plays, because it's a cruel and unusual punishment to heap that responsibility on a green quarterback who is pre-occupied with learning one thing only: survival. Trying to throw a pass while avoiding the pain of getting flattened by hostile rushing opponents is a green quarterback's primary focus. I call the plays for rookie quarterbacks while they learn to beat their fears. After they've grown some, I teach them how to call their own plays one step at a time. First, the quarterback learns how to call a partial play, and eventually, he learns how to call the entire play. After he gets the hang of it, he is expected to call his own plays. There five reasons why this occurs:

1. If he's trained properly, he can do the same job I can within a structured system. If the system includes concrete decision-making models, play-calling can be taught and learned by any coach or player. The system is the solution to play-calling; not one person specifically.

2. He's on the field right where the action is. He's got the best seat in the house to decide what to do next.

3. He has to grow. If I coddle him, his growth stagnates due to the boredom and frustration of knowing that he is willing and able to move to the next-level and call the plays himself, but he's being chained to the past – his rookie past. A veteran quarterback wants to be treated as a veteran, not as a rookie.

4. It's faster. The team can slam it into another gear when the quarterback makes the call, eliminating a time-consuming and potentially confusing messaging system between him and me. Accurate, precise communication is hard enough during a peaceful time. A message can get lost in translation under fire. When I call plays from the sidelines, the opponent has more recovery-time, physically and mentally, giving them a better chance to figure out what we're doing and what they're supposed to do about it.

5. Evidence. Track record. When a finely tuned veteran quarterback has been given play-calling responsibility, our production has always exploded.

This process for my team has never failed. Research and development. Experiment, test, and conclusions. We proved what works for us.

Play-calling is the difference between winning and losing in every profession, in every organization, and every team known to wo/mankind. Play-calling is the minute-by-minute rapid fire decision-making that leads your team in or out of hell. Success or failure in business, sports, crime-fighting, or any other profession is a *chain of decisions*. All success and failure can be studied by *investigating the trail of decisions.* Every win and every crushing defeat can be traced back, decision-by-decision, to learn what worked, what didn't, and why. History doesn't repeat itself. We repeat history when we don't learn by studying past play-calling. Failing to investigate the trail fails to solve the mystery.

There's more bad news about the Decade Rule: if you're not calling your own plays after you've reached expertise, you're not following your calling. You're not on the road to your full potential. You're not on track to becoming who you're supposed to become. Real or perceived expertise may have a seesaw effect. A sinking tolerance leads to a growing frustration. Your tolerance for following plays called by someone else dwindles until it hits zero. Rock-bottom tolerance for following when you're capable of leading causes growing frustration. The frustration of an overlooked leader is not the sign of a shit-disturber. It's the sign of a locked-up veteran soul waiting to bust loose, show his/her stuff, and raise the bar.

The extent of the seesaw effect depends on whether you have an E-soul. If you have the soul of an entrepreneur, and someone else is calling the plays that affect your life after your level of consciousness has been raised past the dependency of the rookie, your E-soul will rebel. Spirited insurrection. Reaching the ten-year mark in policing gave me a bad attitude. My relationship with some bosses and some co-workers suffered. If I didn't see dirt stains, sweat stains, and blood stains on the white-collars around me, my filter shut off. I treated blue-collars with respect, and white-collars with disrespect. My switch broke. The "on" button got stuck. I couldn't walk away from any organizational conflict. Even if there wasn't any, I started some. I got rewarded for being an asshole by getting promoted to detective. I was blessed to learn from some of the very best who gave me play-calling opportunities beyond my wildest expectations. I enjoyed a detective career that I could not have scripted better. However, a white-collar decided to pull the plug after 6 years. My play-calling was taken away. I was dropped to second-string; back to looking at the blue-collar world through the windshield of a cruiser. I was soul-controlled again. A historic event – a repeat of history where I was forced to return to rookie life, re-playing the past, re-runs of tired, old episodes and re-cycling old thoughts. Even though the profession stockpiled more sacred memories than I can count, my mind couldn't imagine thirty or forty years in a workplace that bounces you around a para-miltary organizational chart according to popularity contests, congeniality awards, approval ratings, and the amount of "likes" scored. The thought of not calling my own plays for the rest of my professional life conjured images of hell. I didn't realize then what I know now: these events were supposed to happen. Getting kicked in the ass and knocked down was a message and a push in the right direction. The only force that could drive me away from a profession that I had become obsessed over was the hell of dropping down on the roster.

I left a profession that doesn't have a high turnover rate. About 98.6% stay until official retirement date. Many retire before their official date and keep getting paid just for showing up. The crime of putting in time on taxpayers' dime. I left it behind at the height of my game for one reason only: soul-control. Calling my own plays was more important than the count-down to my pension. I've been asked over and over again how I handle the stress, uncertainty, and risk of changing careers. I've been asked about the finality of leaving behind what has been a big chunk of my life. The answer? Change your perspective. Consider it a warm-up. What you're leaving behind is not the end; it's just an opening chapter. Change is stressful when you look at the past with no future. Never define yourself fully by job, or position, or title, or salary, or any material. All materials are transparent and temporary. Define yourself by what you've become and what you can become. Define yourself by the past impacts you've made and the future impacts that you're assigned to make. A career change is not dropping out; it's moving up to the next level. See the challenge of the future, not the pain and fear of an uncertain future. Focusing on the challenge ahead relieves the pain behind.

Nothing just happens. If you have the soul of an entrepreneur, you will be trained and prepared to start your business in mysterious ways. The key is to solve it. Take time for introspection. When setbacks happen, investigate the trail. Study the evidence that led to it. Put the pieces together. Solve the mystery before you make the next call.

∞

Chapter 21
Accepting the wrong call starts a fire that leads you out of a personal hell, or leaves you burning in one.

I believe that:

- It's a colossal mistake to go into business without having an E-soul.
- It's a bigger mistake to not start a business if you have the soul of an entrepreneur.
- Not following your calling causes conflict inside and out.
- Unresolved conflict is the cause of all hell.

One of the biggest mistakes I made when I started my businesses was bad timing – I waited too long to become a business owner, and I waited even longer to become a *full-time* business owner. I learned a harsh lesson: waiting too long to follow a calling causes the number-one affliction that can kill a business, young or old, and twist your guts physically and mentally: unresolved conflict. Never underestimate the negative power of unresolved conflict. In its mild form, it can stunt growth – yours and your business's. However, advanced cases of unresolved conflict are destructive. They'll rip out your heart and soul. The problem with conflict is that conflict is a problem that needs to be solved immediately; the sooner the better. Make the tough call and change the tense of the conflict from present to past, otherwise, it will carry on into the future, darkening it to the point until you can't see any future at all. We can't predict our future with 100% certainty, but we can envision it. When you can't see any future that's different from today, trouble starts inside. Inner conflict begins to fester. One of the worst inside battles centres on the *wrong call* – state of denial. Not accepting your call. Denying your calling by listening to and following the wrong call.

Beware of the wrong call. The wrong call is a threat to your psychological health and fitness. I believe that your soul has a separate genetic code from your physical DNA. It's a vocational blueprint that won't stop pushing and pulling you in the direction you're

131

supposed to go until you get there. It won't quit on you, will never lie to you, will never mislead you, will never backstab you, will never abandon you, and will never discourage you. However, it also won't take no for an answer. It won't accept losing. It won't let you walk away from your calling, and it won't leave you alone until you listen and follow. I believe that your calling is the ultimate performance demand – no choice, no alternative, and no escape. It's an order that can't be rejected. If you think you can beat your calling, you'll be met with resistance. If you try to follow the wrong call, your soul will apply what looks and feels like punishment, but it's actually intense pressure to motivate you and to make sure that you keep training for what you're supposed to do.

Not accepting your calling is a double-edged sword – it can bring out your worst or your best. If you're not careful, denying your calling can call out your inner beast or tame it. It can cage a monster inside or let loose a monster outside. Additionally, you could go into overdrive, trying to fulfill the potential that you've decided to resist, and fight, and lock up. The difference is how you respond to the inner conflict after you refuse to accept the call.

Unresolved inner conflict has a dark side and a bright side. Unresolved inner conflict is a leading cause of unhappiness, private misery, grumpiness, frustration, depression, exasperation, regression, and all other types of personal hell that goes by different names. The bright side is that it causes change… unresolved conflict *forces* change.

Left unchecked, inner conflict builds the intolerable person who we've all had to face: the asshole. In the mirror or around us, we've all had the asshole encounter. Assholes have a defence – mistaken identity. The reason why we turn into assholes is because of the state of denial. We lose our identity by taking the wrong call. No one is born an asshole. Assholes don't just happen. They're made. They're built because of a frustration for not doing what they want to do. Inner conflict starts the asshole development. The longer the conflict stays unresolved, the bigger the asshole. Investigate any asshole – self or others – and you'll find the exact same cause: emptiness. Every asshole has a void. Unless the void is filled, bitterness builds up and goes to the next-level; mixed-up wiring caused by mixed-up calling. Fill the void and you solve the inner conflict. Fill the emptiness and the asshole disappears. If you're trying to change an asshole, start from the inside-out, not vice-versa.

The downside of the wrong call is giving in and giving up to the pressure to change direction. Giving up and giving in leaves you broken – broken heart, broken soul, and a broken will...*if you choose it.* If you do nothing to change. If you accept the wrong call and live with it. However, there's an upside. Despite its bad rep, an inner conflict of underachieving, of not following your heart, and of not following your soul can be a powerful motivator to change. Inner hell can be the twin-engine booster that propels you to your next level... *if you choose it.* Gut-twisters, like dead-end jobs, can be the most powerful incentives to change. Workplace hell can be a potent motivation that skyrockets you toward your true calling... *if you choose it.* Accepting the wrong call fuels a fire. It can lead an escape from a personal hell, or trap you to burn in one.

If you have found your true calling, this series is still relevant as a cautionary tale – don't mess it up. Don't take it for granted. Don't abuse it, don't disrespect it, don't throw it away, and don't trash it. Protect your calling with your heart and soul. If you have found your ideal workplace that has brought out your very best, this series will motivate you to never make the regrettable mistake of burning your opportunity by killing your calling. If you're doing what you're supposed to do, you're feeling *in place*. You have learned how to *be*. If you have no ambition, desire, or passion to start your own business; don't ever force it...for now. Things could change, but until then, don't start a business unless you're positive that you have the soul of an entrepreneur. I can't imagine starting a business without an E-soul. Two reasons why:

1. I believe it's impossible to fully invest your entire heart into a business without an E-soul.
2. The path you've taken leads to a vocation. That path is your training ground. If you don't have the E-soul, your path leads somewhere else. Wrong path, wrong training.

It's easy for me to say, in retrospect, that you need an E-soul to start a business, but it's much more complicated to recognize what makes up the E-soul, and it's even harder to identify if you truly have one. What does the E-soul look like? What does it sound like? What does it feel like? What are the symptoms? What's the evidence that proves it? The complexity stems from the mysterious way that your soul works. Nothing is clear about the way that the E-soul communicates. You need to become an expert code-breaker because often the soul is a master cryptographer. The E-soul has its own code, its own vocational imprint, and its very own cryptic language. Abbreviations, incomplete sentences, word association, puzzles with missing pieces, stories with chapters out of order, even chapters that make no sense. Mind games. Mixed messages and meaningful messages mixed with meaninglessness. The E-soul doesn't have a conventional voice. It doesn't communicate in ordinary language. The E-soul wants you to work for the meaning, to dig deeper so you learn for yourself how to raise your level of consciousness without having it served royally. The E-soul thinks so far outside the box that the box disappears, which only adds to the confusion when our minds have been trained to accept conventional wisdom unconditionally. Deciphering the soul's messages is part of the endless character-building that we all have to endure to answer our true calling.

I believe that there isn't one generic calling-code. I believe there's no single key to unlock the mystery of the inner workings of the soul. There's no template that we can all use to solve the mystery of what on Earth we're supposed to do next. I believe the best we can do is share our stories with the hope of finding some pattern that will help us open our eyes and ears to filter out what matters and what doesn't.

∞

Chapter 22

If the future is the same tense as the past and present, expect tension.

One symptom of the E-soul is job-fitness. Are you a fit for your job right now or are you a misfit? Are you growing in your job or have your outgrown it? Trying to fit into outgrown jobs is as unsightly as trying to fit into outgrown clothes. Tight tops and floods draw stares, glares, snickers, and whispers. When you outgrow your job, you become a misfit who either sticks out by no longer trying to fit in, or sticks out by trying to fit into a tight space that you've outgrown.

Misfits are caused by a limiting job speed-limit; an uneven growth-rate where you grow faster than your job. When the challenge of a job slows to a crawl, motivation slams on the brakes, and your vision gets blurred – you can't see a future. Acute boredom sets in because of *same reps* – same faces, same places, and same dramas. All this leads to the horror of seeing no future…just a repeat of present and past. When your past becomes your future, your future has past. There is no future if all you see is a replay of the past and the present.

In my case, every paying job I've had reached a point of no-future after crashing head-on into a dead-end. My high school flour mill job turned into a nightmare when I tried to envision forty more years of carrying the exact same flour bags into the exact same box-car. At the 15-year mark of policing, my mind could not picture another 15 years of driving to the same domestics, same bar fights, same break and enters in-progress, same drunk drivers killing and maiming innocent people, absorbing the same pain from the same victims, arresting the same degenerates, listening to the same administrators ignoring the same problems, and listening to the same colleagues gossiping about the same colleagues who are counting down to the same retirement. So I pulled the plug. I made halftime the fourth quarter. Then, the repetitiveness of college teaching shut the light off. I was stuck teaching the exact same curriculum to exactly the same wannabe cops, meeting with exactly the same faculty and exactly the same managers who say exactly the same things to exactly the same problems with exactly the same outcomes. These jobs didn't start off differently. Each job trained me to survive in my own business better than any classroom ever did. I believe I had to go through each job to prepare for selling H.E.L.L. in hell. Without each job, it would have been impossible to understand the complexities of selling H.E.L.L. in hell.

Each one of my past careers had a purpose: they were anabolic agents of character, skill, blue collar work ethic, and street smarts. I learned about the most complex topic on Earth: people. I learned about the reciprocity of impacts; how people made impacts on me and how to make impacts on others. No lesson was more powerful for business than experiencing the power of making impacts on lives. However, each job had an *expiry* date which put ex in front of my job title. I couldn't see a future that was different than the past or present, and I had no control of my future if I stayed until the official expiry date called retirement or death.

On the flip-side, my three non-paying jobs had no shelf-life. Working out, coaching football, and writing were different. I saw a future of growth, challenge, and creativity, and I also saw the autonomy to control them. I needed to find a way to make a living at it.

Before you decide to leave your job and start a business, look into the future first. What do you see? What you can or can't envision is evidence of whether you have an E-soul or not.

∞

Chapter 23
Your future is either scripted for you or scripted yourself.

Script-writing is another symptom of the E-soul. Look into the future and ask yourself honestly if you need a script written for you. Do you need a script to follow? Do you function better with a script that tells you what to say and what to do in every situation? Do you need a script to make every call; even the ones with the game on the line? If the answer is yes to all of the above, don't start your own business, because a self-generated business does not follow a script.

Selling H.E.L.L. in hell is an unscripted journey that needs the skill of *strategizing and improvising* to survive. Unscripted doesn't mean seat-of-the-pants winging-it. It combines *general* planning with the ability to make rapid-fire adaptation when necessary. It requires a general script that needs to be changed without prior warning to solve the unpredictable problems that are part of the business fabric. Improvisation is the skill of structured warp-speed decisions made *within a system.* Rigid scripts won't lead you out of hell; they'll simply lead you to more.

The biggest entrepreneurial myth is the scripted business plan. It is impossible to script a business plan in a volatile world that changes before you finish reading this sentence. The traditional concept of inflexible planning is bullshit. An unchanging script does not deal with reality. You can forecast the future with *some* certainty, but you will never predict it with 100% certainty. The secret is a *system.* A system is a limitless playbook; a structure decision-making model that lets you make the right call at the right time for the right reason without a concrete script. A system is the key to the *cycle of next-level performance.* Systems build people, and people progress alongside the system. Systems move people to the next level. People then bring the system to the next level. Limitless heights are achievable if you're willing to make limitless investments.

If you are unwilling or incapable to make the tough calls in the blink of an eye without blinking, do not start your own business.

You're untrained and unprepared to deal with the reality of being a business owner. Review your past before you decide to start a business. Find evidence of script-writing. Look for experience in writing your own scripts. Has your past prepared you for an unscripted life? Do you need control over your script?

Look into the future again. The type of script you need is evidence of the E-soul. If you're looking for a scripted life, don't start a business. You haven't got the E-soul. If you *need* to write your own script, you've discovered more evidence of an E-soul.

∞

Chapter 24
Unfamiliar and uncomfortable.

Risk is the strongest chain that binds us to our past.

Risk is the strongest barrier that impedes progress into our future.

Risk generates fear of investment of any kind; body, mind, heart, and soul.

Risk represents uncertainty and unfamiliarity leading to mental discomfort, which causes you to pass on opportunities because of P.A.S.S.; Pressure, Anxiety, Stress, and Strain.

Risk is feared because of the wrong focus.

Risk that is not feared is fuel for a greater reward.

Intense focus on risk obscures potential – potential reward, a team's potential, and your personal potential. No risk, no reward. What you focus on grows. Focus on the reward. The reward grows and fear weakens away instead of weakening you. Focusing exclusively on risk will close your eyes to opportunities. It will close your heart to potential, and it will close your mind to even trying because of the unmanaged fear of uncertainty. Uncertainty is the stranger that paralyzes you with fear. Unless you learn to overcome the fear of uncertainty, you will stay in your comfortable shell until you die in it.

If risk terrifies you, do not start a new business, because you will have zero chance of surviving. You won't have a chance, because you will never see all the remarkable chances to succeed. If the word *risk* by itself strikes fear in your heart, you don't have the soul of an entrepreneur. Stay in your job. Don't leave your job, because the true risk is not starting a business; it's you. Being frightened by risk makes you the worst liability to a potential business. No risk is more overwhelming, no risk is more debilitating, no risk poses a greater threat, and no risk is a stronger enemy than a person scared of risk.

Before you make a final decision to start a new business, do a comprehensive risk analysis on yourself. Investigate yourself carefully and honestly to find out what your pain threshold is for risk. No self-evaluation is more important when you're trying to decide whether to become a business owner. Find evidence that you have handled risk before and will handle it again. Then, find more evidence that you haven't formed the habit of running away from risk and that you won't let risk crush you. Build a solid case one way or the other. Do not bullshit yourself. Don't try to fool yourself. Trace your history. Figure out if you've grown some and shown some in the past. There's no shame if you find you fear risk. It's human nature to fear risk.

We've been conditioned since birth to fear any kind of gamble, even if it's not truly a risk, and to doubt your potential. Those are your two strongest enemies: myths of conventional thinking, and self-doubt. We've been brainwashed to fear anything that's outside the comfort of our shell. We've been brainwashed to believe that others are more talented, more skilled, and have more of a chance to succeed. I've seen it first-hand in thousands of student-athletes I've coached. I've seen it in thousands of college law enforcement students. They tremble in the shadow of inferiority; a belief that winning is reserved for others, that they're not good enough to get to the next level, and that they're not smart enough to get hired. Unless they're taught otherwise, their fears only grow until they become a restraining barrier that pulls them away from any opportunity outside their comfort box. If you fear risk, you don't have the E-soul yet. Find a training program first to build yourself up before you make the catastrophic mistake of bringing a new business into the world while you're engulfed in fear.

However, if you have beaten the odds and overcome your fear of risk, you have strong evidence to believe that you have an E-soul. The good news is that you're a candidate to become a business owner because you have proof that you thrive on the challenge of risk. The bad news is that if you don't act on it, you may suffer the consequences. I did. I suffered from two growing conditions: *G.F.I.* and *G.F.Y.*

∞

Chapter 25
Torturing your soul.

You can't have it both ways. You can't flip the risk-taking switch on and off, over and over again. You can't pull out your risk-taking gene and push it back in because it will start an inner domestic dispute that, left unresolved, grows and grows until it spills out in public.

A sure-fire sign of the E-soul is the G.F.I. urge – the **Go For It** desire. G.F.I. is not reckless risk-taking for the sake of gambling. It's challenging the myths of conventional thinking; refusing to be confined by the power of conformity that forces you to make exactly the same, safe call as everyone else simply because everyone says that the same, safe call is the right call because, well, that's just the way it has always been done. G.F.I. is making the call that 98.6% of the world or higher won't or can't make. G.F.I. is the type of call that they call crazy. G.F.I. may get you credit for having some, but many will use *fucked-up* under their breath, referring to the decision itself, and then you personally. G.F.I. causes culture chock. G.F.I. is more than thinking outside the box. It's unconventional thinking so far outside the box that the box disappears. G.F.I. is a counter-culture decision, the type of call that doesn't just defy or break through conventional wisdom but shatters it. The conventional shock-value metre isn't calibrated high enough to measure the reaction. G.F.I. is a seismic shift in thinking that goes through many levels of *oppositioning* – opposition to change your position. Growing intense opposing pressure intended to drag you back inside the box even though it's crammed to its limit.

In my case, I took G.F.I. to extremes in my non-profit careers. G.F.I.s rose in direct proportion to my limitations in my paying jobs. The more I couldn't go for it in my real jobs, the more I went for it in my non-paying jobs. I went from a staunchly conservative football coach to a record-breaking risk-taking football coach. I became the coach who never punted. It became a brand. Probably the only coach in the world who never kicked – no punts, no field goals, no extra-points, and rare deep kick-offs. No one went for it more often; no one went for it in more dire circumstances. I made my

141

own sport by challenging every conventional thought possible that had been passed down through the football ancestry tree. I started a two-decade streak of going for it anywhere, anytime, and anyhow, just to make an impact on my players – to teach them to *never fear being different,* because unconventionalism and original thinking works. I wanted to show them evidence that thinking outside the box makes the box disappear along with your fears of what people will think.

The fear of being different is a killer; it kills drive, kills potential, kills opportunities, kills discoveries, kills growth, and kills your soul. The fear of being different is the biggest obstacle to your creativity; a fictional barrier that you build up in your mind without the drive, or strength, or energy to break it down. Fear of being different keeps you locked up in the standing-room-only box that you won't truly live in…but you will die in. My personal experiment with G.F.I. moments worked. Extreme G.F.I.s translated into next-level performances. Self-esteem, self-confidence, and inner motivation were all the essentials for winning championships. My team's performance skyrocketed because the fear of a pre-conceived risk crumbled. The only fear that was clear was on the other side of the line of scrimmage – the competition fears the go-for-it mentality because of the pressure. G.F.I.s place unexpected, unprepared for pressure on any opponent; an unfamiliarity that builds a crushing discomfort level unless they change their mindset and see it as an opportunity to make an impact by standing their ground and resisting a type of pressure that's a game-changer. G.F.I.s were the proof, the hardcore evidence that going-for-it leads to big rewards. My players didn't just casually buy-in; they reached Level 5 buy-in. Top-grade belief.

The success of my phase 1 G.F.I.s prompted me to raise the bar. I brought G.F.I.s to a higher level. Phase 2 G.F.I. became a strange calling – calling out Goliaths. This meant looking for messes to clean up that others stayed away from. Phase 2 going-for-it became a compulsion to coach the most messed-up teams, messed-up players, and messed-up situations. The worst off the team, the better. Searching out Goliaths and finding the stones to bust them up became a higher purpose.[11] I wanted to make an impact on my players. I wanted them to *always believe in the miracle comeback.* To always believe in the *power of the underdog.* To believe that you can beat the odds no matter how high they're stacked by doing one thing: train harder. Outwork 'em. Stones aren't found; they're built.

It worked, but not without some pain and suffering. Fighting Goliath doesn't always end up in a first-round knockout for the underdog. G.F.I.s taught us two lessons:

1. Goliath is a metaphor for any fear-inducing obstacle.
2. There is a natural struggle needed to beat any Goliath.

There's a step-by-step progression that needs spill-your-guts training; getting in the game and competing hard, falling behind when Goliath takes the early lead, suffering even more setbacks that make the score lopsided at halftime, and the stones to make a miracle comeback. The science of the miracle comeback is the core ideology of self-made business because a start-up business will fall behind on the scoreboard early. No new business takes an early lead and coasts to an easy one-sided win. Every new business will suffer setbacks that will make you not want to come out for the second half. Every new business is a David versus Goliath battle. No new business will score the upset win early in the fight. It won't happen. Every new business will tempt you to fold the team because of a string of bad plays and crushing defeats. To survive in business, you need to believe in miracle comebacks. You have to believe in the *upset.* You have to learn the secrets of making upsets happen. You have to learn how to fight back from losses, from getting clobbered, from getting cut-up, from bleeding so bad that you can't see straight, and from being bruised-up so bad that you can't feel anything but pain.

G.F.I.s are not just habitual, they're part of the E-soul fabric. That's why G.F.I.s spilled over to my two other non-profit careers. I took unconventional approaches to both working out and writing,

---

11   Tribute to a mega-masterpiece: "Then he took his staff in his hand, chose five smooth stones from the stream, put them in the pouch of his shepherd's bag and, with his sling in his hand, approached the Philistine." 1 Samuel 17:40

going-for-it to extremes just to make an impact. I wanted my teams to experience true blue-collar work ethic and *feel* what it takes to outwork your competition. I wanted my law enforcement readers to learn hardcore reality instead of Pollyanna fairy tales. G.F.I.s felt natural; everything was aligned and in place...until I went back to work. Once the G.F.I.-switch turned on, I couldn't shut it off. It became a broken switch. My paying jobs weren't built for G.F.I.s. Large public sector organizations play it safe. Risk-taking is a four-letter word, met with the same enthusiasm as getting a rash. I found out the hard way that you can't turn the G.F.I. switch on and off. You can't play games with an E-soul. You can't let it out and then push it back it.

The easiest way to torture your soul is through a vicious cycle of setting your soul free and then using excessive force to lock it up. It's a cruel and unusual punishment. You'd be better off never letting your soul out. That way you'd never know what you're missing; you'd never experience the freedom, and never feel being completely in place. I learned the hard way that you can't have it both ways. You can't show your E-soul some of the time. Make a full-time commitment to free your E-soul...or hide it completely.

∞

Chapter 26
The extent of fear.

I believe it's impossible to start your own business and be scared of going-for-it, because risk-taking is imbedded in the *soul of an entrepreneur's* DNA. Going-for-it is not an option for the *E-soul;* it's a demand. It's a performance demand to find out what you got and risk what you got. A riskless life is a boring life. Everything worth doing has risk. No risk, no reward. More risk, more reward. The very act of starting a business is as tough a G.F.I. call as you can get because you're putting all you own on the line. There is no such thing as a decision to start a business that doesn't constitute going-for-it.

If you have the E-soul, I believe it won't stay a secret, because you won't be able to suppress G.F.I.s. The G.F.I.-gene will express itself whether you like it or not. It did with me. My G.F.I.s became my scoreboard. I kept score by shock value. I didn't *want* to go-for-it, I *needed* to. Needed it and demanded it. My theory about the G.F.I.-need explains part of the E-soul phenomena – an almost obsessive need for stimulation. The wild search for the next adrenaline rush is connected to one of the most powerful motivators known to wo/mankind: the fear of being bored to death. The E-soul is not merely susceptible to boredom, it's devastated by boredom. The E-soul suffers deep agony from boredom with ordinary life. G.F.I. is a pain-reliever. G.F.I. is a switch that sets off the H-bomb – a flood of highly combustible hormones that kills the pain of abject monotony. G.F.I.s spark the inner fire needed to fight the dullness of routine life. They liven up the deadness of daily regularity automaton existence.

The power of going-for-it goes beyond boredom-busting. There are two more major G.F.I. benefits: *power-branding* and *power-impacting*. Brands are not created equal. There are low-level brands and high-level brands. G.F.I.s contribute to a high-level brand because of the R.E.P.S. factor: **R**are **E**xciting **P**erformance **S**timulates. Doing something that no one else does stirs something deep inside those who don't. Being different sells. Anything out of the ordinary attracts; much like train-wrecks and rubberneckers.

G.F.I. is guaranteed to separate you from the rest. You will become memorable. G.F.I. solidifies a special place in the long-term memory banks of potential customers. The easiest way to build a following is to be different – say something different, do something different, and most importantly, make others feel something different.

R.E.P.S. will push you to a Level 5 brand where you will be safe from mistaken identity – you will never be confused. You'll never be confused about your own identity, and you'll never be confused with your competition. A power-brand is stamped differently; it's cut deeper. A power-brand is indelible. That's the key to a power-brand – permanence. Not all brands are permanent. A weak low-level brand is erasable. G.F.I.s have the force of a drop forge hammer – a G.F.I. brand is built to last. Every G.F.I. separates you from the rest. They make you easy to remember. They make you memorable. The most sacred memories my teams have had, the moments that defined their purpose and gave their experience an upper-level meaning, were the outrageous *"what-the-fuck-is-he-thinking!?"* G.F.I.s that worked. It taught me one of the most potent life lessons that I transferred to business.

Impacts are not created. There are levels of impacts, ranging from low-level impacts that make a temporary difference, to the upper-level seismic shifts that leave an imprint for eternity. G.F.I.s shake a team to its core. They challenge every mental and physical fiber. The heart and soul R.P.M.s floor it into the red zone. The same result happens regardless of whether the G.F.I. moment works or fails – no one is ever the same. No one ever thinks the same. No one ever feels the same about the ordinary. Every G.F.I. moment that failed did two things that transformed teams from misfit, lost-cause underdogs to Davids:

1. Rattled the opponent.
2. Gave us evidence.

Rattling the opponent leads to their unraveling for two reasons:

1. G.F.I.s cause knee-buckling pressure on the competition.
2. The threat of a G.F.I. moment in the future is stronger than actually going-for-it.

The evidence it provided was *how to win.* Studying every failed G.F.I. teaches a secret to winning. No exceptions. When the G.F.I. works, no event has a greater transformative effect. When you make a look-at-what-that-crazy-sonuvabitch-is-doing-now G.F.I. and you make it, well, everyone involved has the stones of David. Stones aren't collected; they're built, and nothing *–nothing –* builds bigger stones than going-for-it; believing it will, *training* for it, and seeing it work. It's like witnessing a minor miracle – you start believing that anything can happen *if you train for it.*

Therein lies a secret to building the G.F.I.-mindset: training. When you've trained for it, go-for-it, because going-for-it is no longer a risk. A risk can be a reckless gamble without any prior preparation. Change the language, change the outcome. When you re-define risk as the *challenge* of doing what you've been trained to do, the fear of risk leaves. Changing the focus, changes the outcome. Shifting the focus from the fear of the consequences to the thrill of the challenge and give your full, undivided attention to the reward. The concept of infinite training-reps is the true secret of conquering your fear. Fearlessness does not come from artificial, superficiality, such as catchy slogans tattooed on skin, t-shirts, wall-posters, or a bumper-sticker. Fearlessness comes from R.E.P.S – the **R**epeated **E**xposure to the **P**ressure and **S**tress of going-for-it after you've worked like a farm animal.

Being untrained and unprepared is not only the true risk; it's a threat. One of the biggest risks to your business is not knowing what the hell you're doing, but going ahead with it anyhow. Delusion. Thinking you're ready but not having immersed yourself in all-out training, having never fully-invested yourself in getting battle-ready, never spilling any guts, or learning what's needed to know to survive. Essentially, there is no such thing as risk; there are only challenges and threats: The challenge of being prepared and taking on a major undertaking, and the threat of being completely incompetent but trying to do it. Challenge or threat, but no risk. Risk is a word that has been handed down through generations by the frightened fearful who try to condition more of the same. That's why going-for-it is rare. That's why it's exciting. That's why it attracts a following.

Teams *love* G.F.I.s because G.F.I.s separate them from the rest and adds meaning as well as *purpose*. Each go-for-it breaks another link from the risk-fearing chain forged by fear-mongers who have paralyzed their potential with the strongest weapon of all: *What if? What if you fail? What if something goes wrong? What if it doesn't work? What if people find out? What if people laugh? What if people think I'm fucked-up?* G.F.I.s make believers from evidence. G.F.I.s turn going-for-it into the driving force that sets the soul on fire – passion. Pure unadulterated passion. My coaching experience has taught about the power of passion. Over 90% of my rookie, lost-cause misfits have had the passion ripped out of their hearts and souls. The transformative power of G.F.I.'s evidence has been irrefutable – train-for-it, need it, demand it.

∞

Chapter 27
Self-doubt.

The most powerful opposition to going-for-it and starting your own business is unchallenged self-doubt. You will have to fight with yourself before you start a business from point-zero. The winner of the fight determines exactly what you'll do with your life; whether you will drain every ounce of your potential, or bury it. Whether you capitalize on your opportunities, or waste them. Whether you live the live you were intended to live, or live some-one else's life. Whether you dictate your professional life, or have it dictated to you.

Self-doubt works in tandem with the wrong perception of risk. Focusing only on the consequences of any decision is an anabolic agent of self-doubt. You'll grow Goliath-sized fears by intensely focusing only on what can go wrong. Dwelling exclusively on the downside will keep you there – on the downside. The more you obsess with what can go wrong, the more self-doubt will stop you from achieving what's in your heart. Policing taught me the solution: *eliminate the worst possible consequence.* From day one at police college, we were taught the golden rule of policing: forecast the worst, and then prevent it. Predict hell, and then stop it from happening. *Professional paranoia;* a survival skill that I've used in every career. It's a powerful decision-making skill that teaches exactly how to build your reality IQ to respect consequences, but never give into them. Consequences have to be feared or you'll suffer them. Fearing consequences is the starting point of preventing them. However, fear is not created equal. There's unhealthy paralyzing fear of consequences that wins the battle of forward progress by building up your self-doubt to a monster that overshadows the truth about your current skills and your potential skills, and then there's healthy motivating fear that drives you to be smart enough to envision all that can go wrong and learn how to stop it from happening.

The operative word is *learn.* Healthy fear motivates you to invest in training to learn the skills needed to beat the consequences and practice them until those skills become second-nature. When you reach the point of automatic performance, your mindset will change. Confidence replaces self-doubt. R.E.P.S are the secret - **R**epeated **E**xercise **P**ummels **S**elf-doubt. Repeatedly practicing and applying any skill beats the side-effects of gnawing self-doubt that, left unchecked, will make you underestimate yourself to the point where you will lose not just a little confidence in your potential; you'll lose all of it. Self-doubt is a belief, albeit a limiting one. Changing a belief doesn't just happen. It needs proof. Repeatedly doing what you thought you couldn't do is evidence that changes the belief of self-doubt to self-confidence. You need to see it to believe it. You need to see yourself working in action to believe what you're capable of.

∞

Chapter 28
Never underestimate the power of self-doubt.

Having an E-soul does not guarantee the guts to start a business from point-zero. The E-soul will not guarantee fearlessness. Even the strongest E-soul suffers growing pains which are inexorably connected to self-doubt. Growth is painful. Growing in your job, your profession, your business, or any relationship is painful because all positive gains have to go through a struggle to see who can cut it; who's willing to earn it and who is not. However, outgrowing a job is worse. Outgrowing a job is more painful than growing *in* it.

The only thing that grew after I outgrew my jobs was conflict – mine and theirs. There's a phrase that's used in the football coaching culture – *uncoachable.* If you Google "synonym for uncoachable" the first one in alphabetical order is *asshole.* Uncoachable is a polite, professional way of saying, *"The guy has outgrown our level of play, it's time to move on, but he keeps hanging around, and he's become an asshole because he's fighting so hard with himself that it spills outside."* I transformed from the model rookie in every job to an uncoachable veteran. I became an unmanageable asshole incapable of taking instruction from anyone because inner hell blurred my vision. Every boss was an asshole simply because I had chosen not to follow my new calling. I fought my E-soul, and everyone paid for it. All trace of self-doubt left in my jobs, but the biggest self-doubt stood in my way – I secretly doubted my ability to succeed as an entrepreneur. I denied it with lies and alibis. I never admitted that I couldn't find the stones to cut the cord from guaranteed public sector incomes. Stones aren't found – they're built. Instead, I chose a new calling to fight the killer boredom of jobs that had abruptly crashed into a dead-end.

As my G.F.I.s grew in my non-profit jobs, I fought anyone who didn't think the same in my paying jobs. If you didn't go-for-it, *if you didn't let me go-for-it,* I labeled you an asshole.[12]

∞

---

12   Tribute to a masterpiece, The Unforgiven. by Metallica. "You labeled me, I label you, so I dub thee unforgiven." Brilliance. Pure genius.

Chapter 29
"And what do you benefit if you gain the whole world but lose your own soul? Is anything worth more than your soul?"
Mark 8:34-38

Go fuck yourself is a vile, repulsive statement. It's gratuitous profanity. It's a manifestation of immaturity. It's an expression of rage and under-developed emotional control. It's a personality defect. *Go fuck yourself* (G.F.Y.) is socially unacceptable behavior and the ultimate form of disrespect. It's contemptuous obscenity. It's an unrivaled insult. It's also possibly a symptom of something deeper: inner demons.

Collisions are not created equal. Fender-benders, to wreckage, to carnage inducing accidents are not equal in scope. Debris is scattered and maybe there's some blood. There might even be an attitude change. G.F.Y. became my new personal mission statement – an occupational philosophy, workplace ideology, and professional core belief. The problem intensified when I started meaning it; and enjoyed it.

G.F.Y. syndrome doesn't just happen. Nothing just happens. G.F.Y. stayed dormant like a hidden virus while I was a rookie, 18 year-old cop. It stayed that way for three years…until my probation ended. The end of the obligatory probationary period was a passage of rite where I got promoted from an entry-level rank that was lower than dog shit in a ditch. Back then, we started as go-for-its – go for the desk sergeant's coffee, go for the prisoners' food, go for gas to fill up the inspector's cars. At the end of probation, the switch broke. Go-for-it turned into go-fuck-yourself. G.F.I. versus G.F.Y. Bad guys, good guys – no discrimination. Then, it spread to the football field as a first-response to any call I deemed uncalled for. First to referees: *"…Unsportsmanlike conduct; 15 yards…"* followed by G.F.Y. It worked its way to opposing coaches: *"…Hey, asshole, you're running up the score…"* followed by G.F.Y. Then, it spread to college administrators. To fit into the world of post-secondary education, I modified G.F.Y.s to a scholarly version, to fit the insular and artificial world of academia. Then, to publishing:

"...I want to change this comma for a period..." G.F.Y. The gym was not immune either: *"...This weight is too heavy..."* G.F.Y.

G.F.I. and G.F.Y. are connected. *"We're going for it."* and *"go fuck yourself."* meant the same thing. They were both ways of silencing inner demons. One prevented frustration, the other released it. However, both were also symptoms of an unsettled E-soul. G.F.I. and G.F.Y. built the strongest case to make the right call. I should have become a full-time business owner long before I actually did. Yet, somewhere in the deep recesses of my brain, I doubted my ability to stand alone as an entrepreneur. I had the wrong focus. I directed my attention to the consequences of leaving security; the security of a familiar job, the security of doing that job really well, the security of the applause for doing that job really well, the security of guaranteed income, the security of not getting fired unless I committed a heinous crime, the security of perceived success, and the security of a painless job. In reality, I sold my soul for $100,000 a year plus benefits. I exchanged my next calling for the comfort of security. I exchanged who I wanted to be for what I was expected to be. Use this as a cautionary tale – don't wait until after your personality has nosedived to make a career change. If you've outgrown your job, and you have a soul of an entrepreneur trapped inside, you have two choices: resign from your job, or resign yourself to a trapped soul. You can't have it both ways. You can't act like an entrepreneur without actually being one.

∞

Chapter 30
Don't let the frightened have their way with your E-soul.

Having a *mind of your own* is a pre-requisite for becoming a business owner. You will need a team to survive, but starting from the time you're trying to decide whether or not to make the leap into the self-generated business world, the essence of entrepreneurial decision-making is the *mind of your own*. Self-made business survival depends on original thinking, not following the leader, because you are the leader. Business survival needs creative thinking to solve unanticipated problems that you can't imagine will happen with alarming frequency after you open the doors to sell H.E.L.L. in hell. However, it's hard to build a mind of your own and to keep it. In fact, there is over a 66% chance you won't.[13] Unless you fight the temptation to follow blindly like a herded sheep, there's more than a 2-1 odds that you will conform to the minds of others. Unless you make a mind-of-your-own happen, you're a leading candidate to get stuck in the crowded traffic jams who follow a leader or misleader. If you want a mind of your own, you're an underdog. The odds are stacked against you. The reason is two forces of nature that are pulling us into the jam-packed box of conventional thinking: risk-aversion and conformity.

One person's excitement is another person's panic. I'm indebted to Dr. Amos Tversky and Dr. Daniel Kahneman. They gave me a legitimate defence for excessive G.F.Y.s. They solved the mystery of my workplace conflict – the battle of safe-players versus risk-takers is real. You can use the defence if you find yourself labeling your bosses as *chickenshit* while they label you a *shit-disturber.* Branding and counter-branding. The doctors' research shows how easy it is for workplace hell to fire up.

In 1979, Dr. Tversky and Dr. Kahneman's research exposed human nature. Humans have a strong desire to play it safe... extremely safe. The majority of humans are L.A.R.A.s - **L**oss **A**verters

---

13   We are indebted to masterpiece studies by researchers Stanley Milgram, Philip Zimbardo, and Soloman Asch that provide compelling evidence of the 66% conformity rule.

and **R**isk **A**verters; safe players. *Loss aversion* means the tendency to make safe decisions that prevent loss over choosing a gain or benefit, that is, playing not to lose instead of trying to win big. Loss aversion leads to *risk aversion*, another programmed preference that avoids a bigger payoff in the face of uncertainty while sticking to an extremely low but certain gain. Choosing a small prize instead of the big trophy. Humans are attracted to playing it safe even when it's the wrong choice. Going out on a limb is unappealing. L.A.R.A.s would rather be wrong than different.

With all due respect to these esteemed scholars, we can reach the same conclusion by working in public sector or watching football coaches in action, where playing-it-safe is a brand. It's a brand so powerful it spans generations and unites people, joining them together to march in lock-step to make exactly the same call in exactly the same situation over and over again.

Safe-players never *go-for-it* except in obvious situations; those backs-against -the wall emergencies where everyone would *go-for-it,* where *going-for-it* is not a choice but a necessity, where *going-for-it* is nestled comfortably in the no-criticism zone. Make sure that everyone thinks alike, acts alike, assimilates into the mainstream, disappears, and *dissolves* into the crowd.

Dr. Tversky and Dr. Kahneman confirmed what we already knew, what we've already seen, and what we've experienced; we fear losing more than we love winning. The pain of defeat is greater than the pleasure of victory. We'd rather flee from uncertainty than fight through it. We are wired to think inside the box, not programmed to think outside the box. We are scared shitless by the big 2 F-bombs: **F**ear of failure and the **F**ear of being different. Then, there is the second-tier F-Bombs: **F**ear of critics, **F**ear of disapproval, **F**ear of being disliked, **F**ear of being alone, **F**ear of isolation, **F**ear of disconnection, **F**ear of not having enough **F**riends (real or computerized), **F**ear of being left behind, and **F**ear of any discomfort; mentally and physically.[14] Eventually, the safe-playing strategy

---

14   Loss aversion and risk aversion are two concepts that were lifted to academic promi-
nence in the landmark study, "Prospect Theory: An analysis of decision under risk" (1979)
by Dr. Amos Tversky and Dr. Daniel Kahneman.

becomes confused for being a rule. The risk-free safe call becomes accepted as law. Eventually, there's an exchange of wills. Freewill is replaced by imposed will. Left unchecked, risk-takers become viewed as violators, offenders of an unwritten code-of-conduct...or just plain crazy.

Safe-playing L.A.R.A.s not only make up the majority, but they recruit heavily. However, they don't have to work hard at it, because the strongest recruiter is built inside us; the potential to conformity. Conformity is a powerful force of nature. Research has repeatedly proven that the majority of humans are followers by nature. Not just ordinary followers, but blind followers. Lemmings. Studies of human compliance gave us the evidence – the 66% rule. A minimum of two-thirds will conform to the thoughts and actions of others, even if it contradicts personal belief. At least 66% of people will not stand up, or speak up or out for what they believe in; a strong case that peer pressure does not vanish at high school convocation. The 66% rule explains our addiction for approval at any cost, including forfeiting a mind of our own. The fear of being different is real; it's intense, and it goes deep. If we're not careful, the potential to blindly conform can overshadow our true potential. The 66% rule proves that having a mind of our own doesn't just happen. We have to fight for it. Unless we take a stand and make a conscious effort and decision to reject conformity *when it contradicts personal beliefs,* we will never experience the pleasure of meeting our true self. If we don't fight the forces of conformity, we'll always be living with a stranger.

The 33% or less who have the mental-armour that protects from conformity have the potential E-soul. Before you make a decision to start a business, do an honest self-investigation by taking the conformity test. Answer the following questions with a score of 3, 2, 1, or 0; 3 for always, 2 for more often than not, 1 for less often than not, and zero for never:

1. Do you do things that you don't want to do to be accepted?
2. Do you make decisions based on what others will think?
3. Do you silence your true opinions when everyone agrees on the opposite?

4. Do you have trouble saying "no" to doing what everybody else is doing?

5. Do you agree with things you don't believe in just to save yourself the grief of opposing others?

6. Do you suppress your true feelings to save the stress of de fending your beliefs?

7. Do you suffer anxiety from expressing exactly what you believe even if the belief is unpopular?

8. Do you hide your true self when you're at work?

9. Do you agree with your boss/colleagues even when you believe s/he is wrong?

If your score is between 17-27, do not quit your job, do not start a business, and do not become self-employed. Seriously, stay in your job regardless of whether you love it or hate it. You don't have the soul of an entrepreneur, and most likely never will.

However, if your score is between zero and ten, the good news is that you likely have the soul of an entrepreneur. The bad news is that if you work for someone else, you will cause and/or suffer conflict. You will probably be a lightning rod for controversy because you're a C.L.A.R.A.: **C**ounter **L**oss **A**version and **R**isk **A**version. You are the anti-safe-player. You're an opponent who will be viewed as a threat, or a risk, or a pain-in-the-ass, or an asshole, or even crazy. Because you're a C.L.A.R.A., you will develop **C**ontempt for **L**oss **A**version and **R**isk **A**version. You will view safe-players as a threat, or a risk, or a pain-in-the-ass, or an asshole, or even crazy. The result is workplace hell because someone is out of place.

I learned the hard way that safe-players and risk-takers don't mix well. Opposing mindsets damage the work environment. In theory, they should balance each other, creating a harmonic alignment – a team in sync. Yet, I've never seen it, because of the Instigator Rule. Risk-takers will instigate controversy because of the speed limit – risk-takers and safe-players don't move at the same speed. I believe that an unfulfilled E-soul won't find peace. It won't allow it, won't work toward it, and won't accept it because of the growth factor. Safe-players and risk-takers don't grow at the same rate. Safe-players don't get worse at the same speed as risk-takers. Unfulfilled safe-players generally stay the same. Although it is possible for safe-players to get worse by playing it even more safe, there's a limit to how safe they can play it. However, risk-taking doesn't have a limit. The entrepreneurial spirit has no boundaries. Therein lies the root of the conflict: C.L.A.R.A.s play to win. L.A.R.A.s play not to lose. The entrepreneur's soul doesn't let the fear of losing get in the way of winning. The soul of an entrepreneur doesn't fear risk and uncertainty; it *craves, needs, and demands* them. The E-soul isn't programmed to play it safe, to make the conventional call, or to run from a challenge. The soul of an entrepreneur is hard-wired with a different program. A L.A.R.A. won't become a C.L.A.R.A., and a C.L.A.R.A. is scared to death of becoming a L.A.R.A. Safe-players scare risk-takers. Safe-players are constant reminders of what a risk-taker never wants to become. That's why peace is elusive. There can't be peace when you fear becoming who you're working with.

∞

Chapter 31
Beware of posing.

It's impossible to take too much time, or go too deep, to discover if you want to start a business. Invest the time to investigate yourself as thoroughly and honestly as possible. Here's another quick test to help you before you make a decision. Simply answer *yes* or *no* to the next three questions:

1. Have you ever tried to fit into a workplace by taking on a wrong shape?
2. Have you ever acted phony at work just to be accepted?
3. Have you regretted remaining silent while pretending to be someone else about a work issue that bothered you to the core of your guts?

If you answered *no* to all three, you likely have an E-soul. It will not give you peace in a controlled work environment. If you're convinced you have it, your soul of an entrepreneur won't tolerate conformist compromise to get out of your calling. I tried, but it didn't work. I attempted to assassinate my E-soul by trying to change my personality, my thinking, my philosophy, and my core beliefs. I tried to hack my E-soul to death by trying to fit in after I realized I wasn't a match for the organizations that I lost faith in.

I have seen and heard some of the weirdest, dumbest, and asinine organizational decisions. The kind of obscure decisions of nightmares that deeply and profoundly affect people's lives. The majority of incompetence I've witnessed was either ignored, like NHL referees turning their heads to flagrant penalties during playoffs, swept under a rug that bulged over, or rewarded by spinning revisionist history, trying to make people believe in make-believe. Rarely were people actually fired. Income was guaranteed, much like untested rookie NFL draft picks. I fought fight after fight until I realized I was fighting no one. There was no true opponent. Instead, there was a system. A culture of what was considered normal. People like me were labeled as abnormal. So, I tried to conform. I gave it my best shot. I started posing. I put on ill-fitting masks and became the pretender. I started agreeing with what I didn't believe.

I stopped fighting for what I did believe. I remained silent, pushing back my true self while my soul kept pushing it out. When two forces collide, a change always happens; guaranteed.[15] The result was hell; a burning hell inside and out because you can't genetically modify your soul. You can try to mutilate it, but you cannot alter your soul's DNA.

Your soul is bullet-proof. If you try to torture your soul, it will torture you back. As much as I tried to choke the life out of my soul by conforming to an unintended life, the E-soul never gave up. The E-soul will never give in just because you lose your heart. Think about that if you decide to put out your fire. I believe, with all my heart, that you will pay the price with more fire; an inner hell that will reveal itself in growing dark spots. Bitterness, resentment, rage, and inner demons will torment not just you, but those around you. Your soul is immortal. It won't die no matter what self-inflicted violence you attack it with. Soul-killing is a myth. If you attempt to murder your soul, it will fight back with a fury previously unknown to wo/mankind. If you don't believe me, look into your past. Remember the hell you've gone through and think of the cause. I'll guarantee that you were not acting in accordance to your true beliefs. When you feel like your soul is ripping apart, it's actually your conscience trying to beat some sense into you with guilt. Your soul is protected by armour. Your conscience does the dirty work of trying to get the point across by any means necessary.

∞

15　Tribute to a masterpiece – the Transfer Theory, a.k.a., Locard's Exchange Theory. Edmond Locard was a pioneer in forensic science. His research proved that an exchange of physical evidence happens during every crime, without exception.

Chapter 32
If you overstay, you're a trespasser.

What kind of an asshole leaves his family and then moves in their basement?

The problem with omens is that they aren't always clear cut. Some don't get to the point. They can be so absurd that they don't seem like an omen at the time the message is sent. Even though an omen may lack clarity and relevance at the moment it happens, eventually it will make sense. It just takes time to sink in. In 1982, the last time a planet *syzygy* happened, where all original nine planets aligned on the same side of the sun, I responded to an *unknown problem* call at a house at 2:00 am on the sixth night of a 7-day midnight shift. If only business imitated policing – imagine your business having a problem you can't figure out on your own that's threatening its survival and being able to simply dial 9-1-1, hang up, and wait for help to clean up the mess. *Unknown problem* calls are exactly like trying to figure out what to do with a career that's hit a dead-end. There's a lot of uncertainty, and you know there's going to be some kind of hell when you get there, but don't expect cooperation from those who caused the problem.

As I parked the cruiser, a woman on the front porch was creatively using *"motherfucker"* as both a noun and an adjective to evict a man from her house. I asked the woman: *"Is he trespassing? Did he break-in?"* She answered, *"No. We're divorced. I want the motherfucker out of here!"* Simple enough. Easy solution. *"Time to go. Come on, let's move."* No one ever listens when they're told it's time to leave. No one cooperates, and no one leaves peacefully when you overstay your welcome; especially a familiar place, the one that has a special spot in your heart. *"No...Not leaving. Don't have to."* And the *"motherfucker"* started to reach into his jacket pocket. Sudden moves during a conflict are always bad moves. Nothing good ever happens when tensions are high and you start reaching. Always listen when someone tells you to stop reaching impulsively. He did, and he asked me to read the letter in his pocket. *"Dear police. This man can live here temporarily. Signed, Family court judge."* Court orders are similar to performance demands; both leave no choices.

"Did he hit you?"
"No."
"Did he threaten you?"
"No."

Being a *"motherfucker"* is not a crime. The man got to stay, even though *mere presence* – the ex-wife, the ex-husband, and the house itself – were painful reminders of the rotten part of the past that was infiltrating the present. Contrary to popular belief, living in the present is not possible unless you have special deleting powers. The miracle of long-term memory won't let you drop the past completely. You can manage the past, but you can't erase it without a trace. The past is made up of sacred moments and hell. They both shape you. The problem is, when you focus only on past hell, it will grow into the present and future. Instead of trying to forget the past; filter it. Let in what you need when you need it. Both good and bad have a purpose. They motivate you at the right time. But at the wrong time, they'll burn you up.

"What kind of an asshole leaves his family and then moves in the basement?" The desk sergeant put down the report later at the police station. *"A glutton for punishment."* was my immediate answer. I had no idea I was forecasting the future. I had no clue that I had warned myself, sending a self-cautionary tale. How was I supposed to know that I played an active role in an omen.

Years later, I quit policing and was hired at my new college teaching job. Construction soon started less than the distance of a football field from my office.

"What are they building?"
"The new police training branch. The entire police force will have to come here all year-round for training."

My ex was moving next door. I saw more of my ex than ever before. My ex dropped by more than ever before. My ex was brought up in conversation more than ever before. I saw what my ex was doing more than ever before. I lectured about my ex. Then I chose to write about my ex. I wasn't just staring at the rear-view mirror; I was in it.

Did I miss policing? No, but with three exceptions: first, when I saw roof lights and sirens after leaving another three-hour lecture of saying exactly the same thing to exactly the same people in exactly the same room. Roof lights and sirens suddenly became attractive again only because I was comparing it to an uglier hell. Beauty is not in the eye of the beholder. It's a point-of-reference. Past hell can look amazing in comparison to current hell. Secondly, after meeting with faculty or administration, my inner child would truly miss the authenticity of a police station where *go-fuck-yourself* is not politically incorrect, where it's accepted, and where it's part of the culture. No one should miss immaturity. Thirdly, when I watched the news or read the paper about some asshole breaking into a house, or robbing old people, or trying to kill innocent people while driving drunk, or stabbing. When I think of assholes hurting innocent people, I miss policing. So, I stopped watching the news and stopped reading the paper. I even stopped watching Hollywood cop shows because the Hollywood assholes looked real. I learned to stop staring in the rear-view mirror, but I would still glance at it when I needed to remember a valuable lesson learned.

If you're thinking of making a career move, you've already made one of three decisions that need to be made. Career changes make seismic impacts. Don't take the decision lightly. Don't make it in a rush. Think it through. A career change needs three total decisions. The first is whether to actually leave a career behind. The second is when. The third is where to go. As soon as you become preoccupied with leaving, you've made the first decision. I believe that working for others has an expiry date *when the challenge goes down and the control goes up.* If leaving your job takes up your time and energy, it's not a coincidence. It's your soul sending a message – new mission and new assignment. However, when is it time to cut the cord? When the relationship is irreconcilable. One sign is hell. If your job becomes an inner hell and you cannot resolve it, the time is up. When you feel out of place and sticking around makes you feel like a trespasser, like an unwanted guest, time is up. Don't wait until you need to be evicted, dragged out kicking and screaming like a protester. I found the first two decisions to be easy. I never had any problem figuring out if it was time to leave and when. The hard part was where.

165

Think carefully before you change careers. Never leave a career until it runs its course. Do not move on until you've drained it. Empty the tank before you leave, or you will live with the deep regret of unfulfillment. Make sure you do what you set out to do. Soak in every minute while you're there because you can't go back. You can't replay it. Ask yourself two questions before you leave it behind:

1. Did I accomplish what I wanted to accomplish?
2. Is the game over?

Never leave a job with unfinished business. Never leave it behind if there's still more to do. Never leave a job with time left on the clock. Make sure there are four zeroes. It's not easy to figure out. Here's how I did it:

In policing, I wanted a decade on patrol, I wanted to be on the S.W.A.T. team, and I wanted to be a big-time detective. In short, I wanted to experience the big leagues. I did *not* want to be the chief. I did *not* want to be a desk sergeant. I did *not* want to babysit a collective bargaining agreement. I did *not* want to be a politician who asked for more money at budget time.

In college teaching, I wanted to get published, I wanted to learn how to teach wannabes how to survive, and I wanted to make an impact by helping misfits fit in and helping lost causes find their cause.

I searched my heart, searched my soul, and knew there would be no regrets. I could see a future. I could imagine a future. That's where I had to go. Most importantly, I never defined myself by profession, rank, or title. If you do, don't leave. The worst type of hell is leaving what defines you. You are the only person who knows the truth. You can get advice, you can get opinions, you can get feedback, but no one can tell you what your soul wants or needs. If your job has run its course, you'll know, because you will not be able to see a future.

∞

Chapter 33
You can't win the fight against self-doubt unless you challenge it.

You can never collect enough evidence. There's no such thing as building a case that's too strong, because even when you've reached near certainty that you have an E-soul, self-doubt will creep in. It always does. Just when you think you've beat your self-doubts, they make a comeback.

Self-doubt is a brick wall. It will stop you dead in your tracks. You won't get past your self-doubts unless you collect enough evidence to prove that you're wrong.

Otherwise, self-doubts will keep making a comeback and put you farther behind. The evidence that needs to pile up is corroboration that you have the E-soul, that becoming an entrepreneur is your calling, that you can't work for other people, that you have to control your own growth, and that becoming a business owner is the only way to gain your freedom and win your independence. Self-doubt and self-confidence are both opinions. They are verdicts. The verdict you reach depends on the evidence you present to yourself, the evidence you focus on, the arguments that you accept, and the arguments you reject.

Just when you think you've convinced yourself to start a business, you will be attacked by a new wave of self-doubts that are stronger and equipped with more intense pressure designed to test whether you've grown some. I used to believe that evil was behind the self-doubts, but now I'm not certain. It might be your E-soul making sure that you've got what it takes to stand up to yourself before you go into a business that will routinely bombard you with one crushing self-doubt after another. Or it could be both. Either way, the secret to beating insecurities is to get to work and find more E-soul evidence. Hard evidence. Concrete, indisputable proof that you are the real deal; an entrepreneurial candidate.

Here's what worked for me. Here's an example of how I built my case that my E-soul was real. I remember five organizational phrases and my instinctive reaction to each one: *chain-of-command, orders, superior-subordinate, people working under him/her,* and *performance evaluations.* They're fighting words. I can't stand them. They make my guts burn. I find each one degrading to the human spirit. These phrases are modern-day feudal language that builds a contemporary caste system. Each one is intended to keep people in their lowly place by robbing them of original thinking. These phrases steal the mind and replace it with someone else's. These phrases are a mind transplant. The best way to control people is by implanting an organizationally-approved generic mindset.

Original-thinkers are organizational nightmares. They scare conventional administrators. As protection, they call their communication system the *chain-of-command*, a psychological ploy intended to shackle your thinking, handcuffing your creativity, opinions, and any desire to challenge institutional dogma. Chain-of-command is intended to break your will to ensure continued surrender to the power of conformity so that you become and remain a 66%er who will adopt anyone else's thinking other than your own. Chains-of-command use *orders* to remove your freewill and securely link your brain to theirs, keeping you in a child-like state of dependent thinking. It's a form of weakness conditioning. Automaton-building through thought de-construction. Zombies. To make sure that the chain-of-command never breaks, and that orders are never questioned, they label the givers and receivers of orders with the most humiliating terms to define organizational relationship – *superior and subordinate*. Nothing – *nothing* – dehumanizes employees more than the title *"subordinate"*. Nothing is more fundamentally ludicrous than using "superior" to describe another human who, in all likelihood, has an equal number of, or more, weaknesses, frailties, and outright dysfunctions than you. Superior and subordinate steers the preferred direction of institutional vision – looking up and looking down. All of which leads to the organizational missionary position – *I have X number of people working under me.* A sign of megalomania. It's a symptom of psychological mayhem; elevating oneself while lowering others because of a title that was likely awarded by nepotism or favouritism in some shape, way, or form.

Once everyone is in place, on top and bottom, then performance evaluations are written. The adult version of report cards, objectively created by veritable strangers who fear anyone perceived as a threat to change positions. Every word written about you, true or false, good or bad, by a designated superior is another link that chains you to a place until the government starts printing your name on old-age pension checks. Performance evaluations are objects of control; extrinsic rewards or punishments that stall the maturation process. Every performance evaluation you sign, good or bad, true or false, wraps the chain tighter. Why? Because you relinquished control. You replaced your subjectivity with a stranger's objectivity. You empowered the evaluator. Report cards are a source of power for the evaluator – *I-know-more-than-you*. They do have a purpose – to guide rookies. To develop the inexperienced. To mentor the protégé. But they build an imbalance of power when performance evaluations are made for the sole purpose of obligation – to fulfill the terms of a collective bargaining agreement. To solidify the position of powerful and powerless.

I found it impossible to fully build and use a mind of your own while chained to someone's command. I was fooled repeatedly by believing that I had been awarded autonomy. Any independence was short-lived. I was simply playing grown-up temporarily. Autonomy was a thinly-veiled disguise for gutless leadership – passing the buck by downhill or zero accountability. I confused independence with the managerial unwilling and incapacity to make the tough calls they were being paid the big dollars for, and the desire to hide instead of seeking the truth. Public sector jobs have a ceiling for original thinking. You smash your head if you try to stand up.

Check your temperature when you hear chain-of-command, order, superior-subordinate, working-under-her/him, or performance evaluation. If they make you boil, you have corroboration of an E-soul. If you stay cool, stay there – you're in place.

∞

169

Chapter 34
The mythical part-time business owner.

Even though I don't get paid for coaching football, I never have and never will use the phrase *part-time* to describe my football coaching career. I always have been fully-invested when I coach football for three reasons: it's my passion, it sends a dangerous message of indifference if not fully-invested, and part-time commitment always ends up in losing.

Even though I didn't get paid for working out, I never have and never will use the phrase *part-time* to describe my strength training career. I have always been fully-invested when I lift because part-time commitment always ends up quitting when the pressure gets too tough. It's too easy to walk away when you're not fully invested.

I never used the term part-time police officer or part-time college professor, but I used *part-time* business owner when I started my businesses. It was a dumb-ass decision. Among all the stupid business decisions I made, none were worse than calling myself a *part-time* business owner. Never call yourself part-time anything, because it guarantees a loser mindset; a failure mentality. An attitude that breeds incompetence and irresponsibility through neglect.

The psychology of *part-time business owner* could fill a separate book. It goes by different names such as *business on the side,* like an order of dripping, greasy fries. *Part-time* is your personal contract to be half-assed, to not commit, to justify done-and-run, to create something, hand-off the responsibility of raising the business, vanish, and re-appear when the heavy lifting's been done, when there's an applause, and when it's time to take a bow. Appearance by convenience. *Part-time* sends a message to you, to your staff, and to your customers that are not fully invested, that your true focus is somewhere else, and that your business is not your top priority, or your true passion, or your true love. It could also be interpreted by you, your staff, and your customers that you're a deadbeat business owner who doesn't give a shit about your business, so why should anyone else? Identifying yourself as *part-time* means that something else is more important. Here's a key: either you are a business owner or you're not. There's no middle ground. Full-time business owner doesn't mean you can't do anything else, but it does mean that *full-investment* is compulsory for full return. Change your language, change the outcome – eliminate *part-time* from your vocabulary, and your business performance will automatically and instantly change.

The root cause of the *part-time* label is self-doubt. Fear of commitment stops you from becoming a full-time business owner and even saying it. You'll think you can do it on the side. You can't. There's no such thing as a part-time business owner. A business on the side will never get out in front. It will stay on the side until it drops dead last. Your business is a full-time venture. Either you are full-time or you aren't. Part-time is part of the *entrepreneurial delusion;* the illusion that the business will either raise itself, or someone will raise it for you. Part-time is not just the chicken-shit way out, it's abdicating your responsibility to your creation. Full-time does not mean you have to work in your business – players play, coaches coach; not vice-versa. However, it *does* mean that you have to be the leader. The head coach. The play-caller who designs the system, the playbook, the philosophy, the language, and the one who makes the calls until your field general learns to make them and not a moment too soon.

Part-time is irrationalization that makes you feebly justify to yourself that part-time attention is smart. That it will work. That it's the right thing to do. *Part-time* is an escape from reality, hoping. wishing, and convincing yourself that wrong is right. It's worse than a defence mechanism; it's an attempt to bullet-proof yourself by never seeing the battlefield. Flight instead of fight. The worst part of being a self-appointed part-time business owner is the bloodbath that is guaranteed to follow. Sending an unprepared team into battle is unconscionable. It's foolish, inept, and a clear failure of character.

But what if it does work? What if part-time gets the job done? Then it wasn't part-time. If your business becomes a 10%er, a Darwinian survivor that becomes built to last, then you *have* been fully invested. If you want to make your self-generated business succeed, fight conventional thinking. Don't believe the part-time myth. Part-time business owners don't succeed by any definition of the word. At best, they just hang on.

∞

Chapter 35
There's low population at high altitudes.

What do you do in the face of danger?
What have you done in the face of danger?

The answer to these two test questions will answer the third question – *what will you do in the face of danger?* If the answers show you're a runner, don't start a business. If you run from problems that threaten your team, stay in your job so that you will have people to solve them for you. You don't have the E-soul. However, a perfect score is strong evidence that you have it. The E-soul is not a runner – it doesn't run away from danger. It thrives from it. The E-soul wants to solve big problems that threaten the team. *It needs it.* This isn't just a motivational speech, and it's not an ego-booster. It's a cautionary tale. You can't survive in business if danger makes you run. If you don't have a history of standing up to danger and fighting through it, stay in your job. Spare yourself grief and heartache. Do not start a business now or ever. I can't downplay the necessity and power of an E-soul and being *fully-built* by it.

Being fully-built by the soul of an entrepreneur doesn't just happen. I believe the E-soul brings us along slowly from infancy and keeps strengthening us toward our full potential despite our resistance, uncooperativeness, our petulance, our immaturity, and our outright rejection of the growth opportunities, those scared moments that we squander because of laziness, fear, or both. Being born with an E-soul will not guarantee the fearlessness to stand up to threats and fight through danger. We have to be fully-built by the E-soul through the promise of a pathway that teaches how to work out the traditional fears that control your flight-or-fight switch, pushing you to run the wrong way.

Do not try to sell H.E.L.L. in hell unless you have hardcore evidence that you have full control of your fight-or-flight switches. If your running switch controls you, don't do it. If you're a runner, do not attempt to sell H.E.L.L. in hell. Play it safe by the conventional definition of safe. That's not an insult; it is concern for your financial security and your sanity. It's impossible to sell H.E.L.L. in hell if your flight switch has been stuck in the "on" position. Before you jeopardize everything you own, find out if you control your running switch or if it controls you.

Danger in business can be found in many places, but the two most common places are in the dark and at new heights. If you are scared of the dark, don't start a business. If you're scared of heights, don't start a new business. Here's why: new businesses will guarantee dark moments. Pitch-black moments where you can't see anything, can't hear anything, and can't feel anything. Examples of the dark include, but are not limited to:

- Your primary customer-base hates buying what you're selling.
- The city where you open a business economically collapses.
- The government funds a Goliath competitor, tilting the playing field by opening a business with endless resources including public taxes that you're contributing to.

If you can't find your way out of the dark, don't start a new business. How do you know if you can? The past. Check the past. Is it checkered or not? Have you walked into the dark? Did the dark scare the shit out of you? Have you escaped the dark? Have you ran? Closely examine every dark moment and analyze your reaction.

Darkness is the expected danger, but lofty heights aren't because, on the surface, it seems that reaching new heights is what you're aiming for, so it's seemingly a comfortable place. It's not. Coaching football taught me that first place is not only an elusive place to get to, but it's even harder to stay there because of a psychological phenomenon – fear of falling and fear of failing. New heights are scary because they are foreign, lightly populated, and if you look up or down, the same thing happens – self-doubt attacks. As you climb level by level closer to the top, you get a feeling that you don't belong there because you've never been there. What is unfamiliar also frightens. Success, even one level at a time, isn't easy to handle. Questions start popping up in your head. Am I worthy? Can this last? *How* can I make it last? What if we start to slip or free-fall? Every climb to the top causes fatigue, a new kind of fatigue – altitude fatigue. An advanced debilitating fatigue that you've never experienced before. Unless you've trained for altitude fatigue, it'll crush you. Reaching new heights is a struggle that is intended to weaken those who can't cut it and strengthen those who can.

There's plenty of room in the dark, and even more room at the top, because 98.6%ers run away, and 1.4%ers run toward both places. Very few want to get there, need to get there, and will fight the struggle long enough to get there. 10%ers *may* have the willingness and capacity to separate from rest. 1.4%ers will. The others will simply get stuck in the traffic jam.

∞

Chapter 36
Read the signs.

I drove past signs. I never stopped once to read any of them. I knew they were there. I saw the blur and felt their presence, but I never took the time to read any sign in its entirety. I kept missing one of the biggest signs that it was time to become a full-time business owner – contempt for being micromanaged; being professionally controlled by another adult who may be incapable of running his/her own life let alone trying to run mine. It took me too long, but I eventually and finally recognized it.

Micromanagement is leadership by complete control – pure 100% unadulterated control. It's the equivalent of the strict parental supervision of a child. Micromanagement is needed for rookies, those entry-level time-bombs who need to be controlled, not just led. Generally, rookies are loose cannons ready to explode, fire, or misfire at the first sign of real or manufactured stress. Therein lays the purpose of micromanaging – to straighten out delusional rookies who believe they have made it without having made anything happen whatsoever. However, micromanaging loses its purpose when erratic rookies straighten out. Micromanaging is a growth-killer, a catabolic agent that weakens and builds only one thing: the need for continued dependency. Micromanaging is counter-productive and counter-intuitive. It's professional stalking. Obsessively and excessively looking over the shoulders of seasoned veterans is a symptom of a bad problem; a system failure. Either the veteran never actually grew up because of incompetent training, or the micromanager cannot control a deeply imbedded psychological problem rooted in distrust – not trusting the team, not trusting the training, or both. Either way, it's a sign of insecurity. The micromanager is suffering from a character void carved out by the dreaded feeling of inferiority brought on by the terrible truth that they really haven't been on the frontline, have never gotten their hands dirty, and have never seen the action that they are trying to manage. Inferiority and micromanaging are intimately connected – those who have never done it try to mask it. Micromanaging is a diversion and compensation, a diversion from the truth that one's team has more of what the manager doesn't; more experience, more knowledge, and more moxie. Micromanaging is compensation for never having grown or shown some big enough. Micromanaging grows from the absence of self-confidence. The micromanager's insecurities spread to the team, infecting it with the underachieving virus. A micromanaged team operates under a low ceiling, cramming it and jamming it in a tight space, making sure it never stands up for itself.

Veteran micromanagement is a red flag. If you have earned your spot as a first-stringer after years of proven performance, and you're still under the microscopic eye of a manager who can't give you the keys to the car, you will never become what you're capable of becoming because of *suppressed discretionary authority;* the locked-up talent of accepting and executing responsibility. The difference between winning and losing is the balance between automaton-assignment and discretionary-assignment. Both have distinct purposes in winning big. Both are needed to win big. You can't earn the trophy with just one or the other.

Automaton assignment is discretion-free work – non-negotiable, no room for change, and no option for improvisation. It's robotic, machine-like performance. There's no responsibility. There's only accountability. There's a big difference between these two concepts of accountability and responsibility. Accountability is the obligation to be counted on by your team to do exactly what you're told to do, performing the task the very best way you can. Accountability is the willingness and capacity to follow orders and to carry out performance demands with military-like precision. Responsibility is decision-making authority – the freedom to *make* the call when it's time to call a play or *change* the play that was called before the action starts or while it's even in progress. Responsibility is one of the most potent motivators *when it's given at the right time.* If you want to motivate someone, give them the responsibility to call a play *at the right time.* If you want to make someone feel important, give them the responsibility to call a play *at the right time.* If you want to show your trust, give them the responsibility to call a play *at the right time.* If you want next-level performance, give them the responsibility to call a play *at the right time.* If you want to win big, give them the responsibility to call a play *at the right time*. However, if you want to crush some, give them the responsibility to call a play *at the wrong time*. If you want to get your team clobbered, give them the responsibility to call a play *at the wrong time*. If you want to end up dead last, give them the responsibility to call a play *at the wrong time*. When's the right time? When it's earned. When there is proof during simulated training that they've learned it and earned it. It's the right time when there's evidence during practice that they can accept responsibility. It's the right time when they follow it up with evidence during a game – when the action is live and when it counts.

After rookies grow up, learn the ropes, and are no longer threats to team survival, they need discretionary authority and some leeway to call their own plays. If rookies are taught and trained effectively, they will *need* to call their own plays. They won't just want to; they'll need to. It is part of the natural growth cycle of any employee, any performer, and any team player. Otherwise, they remain rookies forever, stuck in professional childhood intellectually and emotionally. Psychological immaturity. A veteran who needs to be micromanaged is an oxymoron – s/he is still a rookie…and likely always will be.

Micromanaging becomes a power-play when it's used to hold back veterans whose leadership and expertise become a threat to misleaders disguised as leaders who feel inferior and insecure because they lack what their team has; the expertise of the veterans they are leading. Contrary to popular belief, knowledge is not power. Knowledge is the fuel for power. True power is practical experience – applied knowledge. What you have done with knowledge and what you are doing with it is purest form of power. Knowing how to do something is the equivalent of a full tank of gas. Actually doing it takes drive. Putting it in motion means turning the switch and pushing the pedal. Practical experience is a force of nature and nurture. Stored knowledge isn't. Practical wisdom trumps theoretical wisdom. Street-smarts beat stored-smarts. There are two kinds of managers – those who have done it, and those who didn't. Those who have done it know the secret of building power – individual power and team power – by sharing it, teaching it, and coaching it.

You build up yourself by building others. Unfortunately, those who haven't done it resort to stealing power – petty thieves. Micromanagement is the only strategy of the inferior to horde power from those who have done it. The only way for unaccomplished, unqualified micromanagers to become powerful is to make others powerless. True leaders build power by building the powerful. True power is the power-exchange, not the power theft. The difference between first place and last place is how powerful your team is, not how powerful the leader is. Shared power wins; isolated power loses.

Granted, some rookies never grow up and arguably need micromanaging for their entire career because of training failure where the message didn't get through – either the rookie wasn't taught right, or the rookie simply didn't catch on. Some rookies have no desire to leave the dependency of micromanagement. In defence of micromanagers, independence frightens many people. It traumatizes them. They chose a career of dependence. In those cases, micromanaging becomes a team survival mechanism. Those who don't want to grow up need to be micromanaged or cut. In the case of the slow-developing veteran, micromanaging is a back-to-the-drawing-board solution for performance that failed to grow – it's re-training. However, in the case of fully-grown, fully-functional veterans, micromanaging is a chain that tries to drag the veteran back in time, all the way back to rookie days. In those cases, micromanaging has no purpose other than to keep solid, proven veterans in their lowly place on the tail-end of the chain-of-command. When micromanaging happens after you've proven to have gone to the next level, it's an alarm – an intrusion alarm. It's psychological invasion. When the alarm is activated, a choice has to be made: accept or reject micromanaging.

Accepted veteran-micromanagement is a sign of a career slamming on the brakes or shifting into reverse. If you've earned the right, *and* then are rewarded by being treated like it's your first day on the job, *and* you accept it without any challenge whatsoever, you've dignified the micromanagement. Rewarded it. Fueled it. It will only get worse. You'll go back in time to becoming the same green, wide-eyed rookie who was stuck under a microscope. Unless there's a change, a micromanaged veteran will suffer conflict, cause conflict, and spread it. Accepted veteran-micromanagement is the biggest sign of surrender. If you surrender, you also give up your originality, your creativity, your truest self, and you lower the level of consciousness that you spilled your guts for. If you accept micromanaging, you brought it on – you brought on the mask, brought on the pretending, brought on the game-playing, brought on the inner hell of locking up your dignity, of burying your talents, of wasting your experience, and wasting a future that you no longer can see.

Like many people, I've experienced the management pendulum – the extremes of life-changing mentors to incompetent, micromanagement. I've been blessed to have been mentored by hall-of-famers. Legends. However, I've also been cursed with micromanagers who tried to genetically change anyone who did not fit the company model. Genetic modification is the misleadership goal of the micromanager. It brings everyone down to exactly the same level; the lowest possible level. The gutter.

I never accepted it. Not once. I fought it each time. I won each time. Undefeated. But that was the *worst mistake of my professional life*. The endless fight against micromanagement is a colossal waste of time and energy for three reasons:

1. Micromanaging is like a vampire. You can't kill it. It never goes away. The pendulum will always swing from the great leaders who will lift your soul to unimaginable levels of consciousness and performance, all the way back to the bottom of the barrel. Any change you effect by winning a fight is temporary. Nothing changes permanently while you're working for someone else. Like chronic acne, another micromanager pops up just when you think it's finally cleared up.

2. Freedom is addictive. When you win freedom, you'll never accept control. You will fight even harder each time another dictator comes along until you become a monster.

3. In my case, the time and energy I invested to win each fight set me back in my development, growth, and training as an entrepreneur. I delayed the inevitable. I had the chance to become a full-time business owner on several occasions, but chose instead to fight unsanctioned fights, meaningless fights that lead to nowhere. Not one victory led to positive change, to self-improvement, or to team improvement. The conflict was never truly resolved; not the inside conflict and not the outside conflict. Unresolved conflict is the leading cause of failure, of losing, and the worst form of torturing the soul. Every battle won wasn't a victory. It was another defeat by interfering with my growth, my worldview, and most of all, my next calling.

I learned a valuable lesson the hard way. If you don't like being micromanaged, resign. Resign yourself to micromanaging, or resign from your job. There's no fight. The only fight is with yourself. There's no opponent when you're working for someone else. If you have the soul of an entrepreneur, the fight against micromanagers is senseless. It's foolish because it's impossible for the soul of an entrepreneur to light on fire in someone else's organization.

The stream of great mentors in my life was not a coincidence, and neither were the micromanagers. I don't believe in coincidences. I believe in connections. One event is connected to another. Everything that happens has a purpose: to react to it. To make the next call. Every play, good or bad, is a link in the chain of events that will shape our lives. When one play ends, we have to call the next play. I believe in the *E-spirit*, the entrepreneurial spirit that works in tandem with your soul and conscience to *open a hole*. They choreograph every play by blocking, and tackling, and hitting, and cutting down what's in the way to open a hole. Some will be big enough to drive a truck through it. Others are a sliver of light that you have to squeeze through by hitting it hard and fast before it slams shut. Some plays are unmitigated disasters where you can't find the hole, get sacked, and might even get busted up and shed some blood. Some are game-changers. But each play sets up the next call, which is unavoidable. Even if you choke and don't actually make the call, you still called a play: nothing. Calling nothing is still a decision, and a choice that will change the game.

My misguided fight against micromanaging for freedom and control broke speed limits. It was distracted driving. I was too preoccupied to read the same sign that I kept driving past – get out, start your business, and *invest 100% in your business for maximum return instead of investing 100% in useless fights to get no return.* Not by coincidence, what finally made me a full-time business owner was the last pendulum swing – a new micromanager; the strangest, most unusual micromanager I had ever met. It was a new layer of hell. It was the equivalent of sliding one plate too many on the bar. No matter how strong you are, there's always a *threshold plate*; that one plate that forces you to put the bar down. That one plate that makes the weight too heavy to lift. The threshold plate doesn't have to be big, or heavy, or challenging. By itself, the threshold plate is a lightweight. It's insignificant. But when you add it to the rest of the big plates, it becomes the heaviest-weight; that one that goes past your personal best, and the one that no longer makes you strong. The proverbial straw that broke the camel's back.

The straw, in my case, was an asshole. Nothing extraordinary to write about. Just another boss trying to make his mark – piss on the fire hydrant because he knows no other way. One asshole is enough. One is easy to handle, but when they multiply, things get nasty. The saturation point is reached. Nothing just happens. Assholes are sent into our lives for a reason – to move us. Send us in motion. Free us. The key is perspective.

∞

Chapter 37
Look for what will make others rich quick.

The purpose of entrepreneurism may seem to be to make money, but it's not. Making money is a by-product. The true purpose is to make an impact on people. If you make an impact, you'll get rich quick – inside and out. If you don't, you won't. You'll go broke – inside and out. It's the same with any job. What separates superstars from bench-warmers is the extent of impact made. Everything else is secondary. Find the missing impact, focus on it, and make it happen repeatedly – there's a key to success by any definition you want to give it. Jobs, sports, fitness, business; make an impact, doing it over and over, and success is guaranteed.

Detective work taught me how to follow the leads to find out who did what, but coaching football taught me a fantastic way to follow the leads to turn losing into winning. I learned the value of *film study*. Videotape each game and investigate every play – why they were called and how they were executed. That research finds every single piece of evidence needed to win in the future. The secrets of future success are in the past. Go back in time – fix what went wrong, and build on what went right. Re-playing the game for the sake of entertainment is a waste of time. Agonizing over a crushing defeat or celebrating a big win won't cut it. Studying for clues will unlock the mystery of what to do next.

Following the leads is critical to making every entrepreneurial decision to avoid the broken heart of a broken business; starting with whether or not to open a new business or scrap the idea. Then, if the evidence proves you've got the E-soul, and you're ready to become your own boss, there are two more critical decisions to make: what are you going to sell? Where are you going to sell it? Follow more leads, but don't make the mistake of looking for what will make you rich quick; look for what will make others rich quick. *Making others rich makes you rich.* Make people rich emotionally, intellectually, physically, spiritually, and psychologically. Enrich their lives, enrich their experience, enrich their outlook, enrich their wellness, enrich their well-being, and enrich their day-to-day existence. Enrichment is an abstract concept and complex dynamic, but it's founded on one simple truth: make it better. Improve lives, improve the reward, improve the meaning, and improve the thrill. Improve the mind, improve the body, improve the soul, and improve the spirit.

The conventional definition of *rich* is the biggest barrier to happiness and self-fulfillment. If you define rich solely by a financial concept, you will end up empty. Psychologically bankrupt. Emotionally withdrawn. The reason is that financial success by itself does not make an impact on anyone but you. Monetary riches that don't enrich lives will lead to emptiness and a psychological void because no amount of money earned can outdo the greatest reward: putting up ladders for others. Giving others the opportunity to get to the next level, to help them reach their potential, and to dramatically change lives is the single most greatest reward that can be experienced.

When it came time to decide what I wanted to sell and where, I followed the leads. I connected all the evidence I could find from the past. I decided to do what I did best: lifting. **H**eavy **Ex**treme **L**abourious **L**ifting; physically and intellectually. H.E.L.L. Working out, football, writing academic textbooks. Coaching and teaching thousands of wannabes. Instructing lost souls who wanted to make a difference. I followed the leads even more. I connected more evidence. The impact has been immeasurable. It's off the charts. H.E.L.L. had dramatically changed countless lost souls consistently. H.E.L.L. was the secret formula that turned around lost causes. H.E.L.L. had lifted point-zeros from their personal hell. The evidence proved my case beyond reasonable doubt. That's how I decided to sell H.E.L.L. in hell. Lifting lost souls and turning them into souls of lifters was what I did best. I decided to sell H.E.L.L. exactly in the places I knew inside-out: hell; the most difficult place to succeed in business. Why? Three reasons:

1. Not many will try to compete in hell.
2. Not many can stand the heat in hell.
3. Hell has potential *if you understand the mindset of hell, if you can help others escape from hell, and if you can make people forget where they are.*

Rich is an unintended concept. Both companies let my children and their children live unrestricted lives. I never once gave my grandchildren a thought when I started my businesses. I was simply trying to escape hell – the hell of not doing enough, the hell of job monotony, and the hell of poisoned workplaces that put my soul, spirit, and conscience under constant attack.

∞

Chapter 38
Winning is not a crime.

Winning is not a four-letter word. Never apologize for wanting to win. Like anyone or anything that gets labeled with a bad rep, winning is misunderstood. It's the subject of myth. False allegations are born from tunnel vision, the fine art of manufacturing evidence and magnifying it while shutting out anything that we don't want to hear. Disregard and delete what doesn't fit; scratch what doesn't match. Block out what doesn't confirm our suspicions.

Those who want to de-emphasize winning generally fear competing. Specifically, they fear the *natural struggle* needed to compete and to win at any level; in business, sports, professional and personal life. The natural struggle is the unavoidable fight that has to be fought to get to the top. The lack of will and capacity to endure the struggle needed to win is compensated for and masked by de-emphasizing winning. Those who can, do; those who can't, de-emphasize it. Downgrade it. If you can't or won't do what it takes, make it less important. Downplay what you can't play.

The de-emphasis of winning is a psychological ploy for *pain-averted reward,* that is, averting the pain of last place without earning it. Guaranteeing a spot in the standings without the pain of the natural struggle. The entitlement of unearned pleasure. Every win is the product of a struggle. You can't win at anything without enduring struggle, and nothing is worth winning if no struggle is needed. You can't call anything a win if you don't have to fight tooth-and-nail for it. Every struggle is uncomfortable. All struggle causes pain that has to be managed, conquered, and worked through. *Crush or be crushed.* Therein lies a true challenge of winning – crush the struggle or get crushed by it. Which pays out the reward bigger than any trophy, bigger than any championship ring, and bigger than any medal? The inside job; the inner reward. Testing yourself day in and day out by not breaking, not giving in, and not giving up. Lasting. Built-to-last never finishes last. That's how we grow by beating one struggle at a time.

Opponents of winning want to deprive everybody of the top prize, the experience, the growth, and the *feeling* of winning by eliminating the struggle. By-pass it. They don't want to end up in last place, so they advocate its abolition. Get rid of first place and last place, leaving everyone tied in the middle of the pack, thereby eliminating the dreaded Darwinian process; allowing the weak to progress while making the strong extinct. No one has to worry about getting better, no one has to be concerned about potential, and no one has to worry about being different, because no will be allowed to. Sameness hides the hurt of not winning.

Advocates of de-emphasizing winning miss the point. Winning is not evil, because winning is a *by-product* of dedicated training, not a Machiavellian objective that is obtained by crime, by offense, by insult, or by sin. Winning is an *outcome* of noble, honourable work and exertion. The only true evil associated with winning is *pressuring someone to win without working for it.* Expecting the best without giving your best. If an obsession for winning bothers you, shift the focus. Change the focus, change the outcome. Re-define winning. Change the perspective. Teach kids the *value of commitment* to work, to training, to practice, to skill development, and to do all of it both alone and within a team. *Don't even mention winning and you'll get a healthy outcome; an intrinsic reward of accomplishment regardless of whether they win or lose.* Experiencing full commitment is explosive and transformative because it's the truest accomplishment. It's raw achievement. Sticking to something that's hard to do tells you the most about who you are. It tells you more than anything that anyone else can tell you. Sticking to it, not giving in, and not giving up is the ultimate polygraph test of self-analysis. It tells you the truth about who you are. There's zero chance of error.

De-emphasizing winning is dangerous because of deprivation; we would all lose the benefits of *trying to win.* The *attempt* to win is a key that can't be lost. The *attempt* is what builds strength. The *attempt* to win is the growth process. De-emphasizing winning teaches a false reality; the delusion of trying to achieve without going through the process, and without investing in the intense training that leads to winning. Winning is simply the reward for enduring the journey. That's why winning is not evil, nor is the desire to win. A passion for winning is a basic survival need and shows a healthy, realistic mindset. It shows the tireless, workwo/manlike work ethic needed to survive in real-life. That mindset shows you're dealing with reality rather than escaping it.

If winning is de-emphasized, losing gets lost in the shuffle, and with it goes the *value of losing.* The secret to success is woven in the fabric of losing. *The formula for winning is learned by studying losing.* Success by any definition is corrected losing. Regardless of how you define it, a secret to success is discovered by *investigating failure* and then making it happen – experience failure, solve the mystery by finding the evidence of success in failure, and execute what you learned . De-emphasizing winning is an injustice, depriving young people of the most important education that will shape their future, build their potential, and let them reach their destinies. Sheltering young people from losing is a form of academic neglect and educational fraud. It's not only misguidance, but it is *misleadership.* Coddling young people by protecting them from failure keeps young people weak and immature. It stagnates their growth, leaving them powerless and fragile. Give young people more credit – they can handle more than you think. Don't take away their chance to handle adversity.

Losing is painful. If you are a good sport and accept losing, do not start a business. You don't have an E-soul if you have a high tolerance for losing. If you are not ultra-sensitive to losing, spare yourself suffering – work for someone else. Do not jeopardize your financial life. Don't start your own business. De-sensitization to losing is a guarantee for business death. The reason is fire extinguishing; you will not have the fire to make the miracle comeback, a pre-requisite skill for business survival.

Stamped in the heart of the E-soul is the will and capacity to win, the refusal to accept losing, and a flat-out contempt for giving in, giving up, and forfeiting the game to your competitors. That takes scorching heat. Scorching temperature. A soul on fire. The E-soul operates past the boiling point. Before you decide to become a business owner, check your temperature. Don't fool yourself by thinking that starting a business is merely an escape from assholes and workplace hell. Honesty in, honesty out. Escaping your job is not enough to last in your own business. The will and capacity to win big is a non-negotiable trait. Winning *big* needs the *perfect-season mindset.*

Coaching football taught me about the miracle of the *perfect season – undefeated.* An unblemished record. It's the boldest statement your team can make. *Perfect season – undefeated.* No statement packs a bigger competitive punch than those three simple words. It's worth far more than one-thousand words. *Perfect season – undefeated* sends the perfect message to your competition, to potential ticket-buyers, to potential advertisers, to recruits, and to the media. *A perfect season shows your heart and soul to the world.* It covers everything you want to communicate, from your expectations to you team's capacity. It has drawing-power. "Perfect season" attracts with an unnatural power by conjuring an image of the purest form of excellence. A three-word statement replaces an encyclopedic narrative about who you are, what you've done, and what more you're capable of doing. Nothing elevates your credibility higher and faster. It travels at the speed of sound. No words spread farther and faster than doing something rare. Doing something different is jet fuel for word-of-mouth travel.

After our first one, I typed *perfect season – undefeated* at the top of our team goals. It was the number-one objective on the list. Two reasons why: because it says it all, and because it can be done. It's possible to build a long winning streak, but winning streaks don't just happen. Winning streaks don't happen by luck, or good fortune, or by magic, or by hoping, or wishing, or sending positive vibes out into the universe. Winning streaks take an investment of painful work to avoid the pain of going broke. You have to put your heart and soul in it.

My biggest business mistake was not typing *perfect season – undefeated* at the top of our business goals from day one. Epic failure. The harshest lessons we learn are often what was obvious – what we already know. Never feel guilty for your red-hot passion to win. Do not cave in to the pressure of misguided bleeding-hearts who want to drop in the standings and join them in the crowded box of mediocrity. Never conform to those who fear the struggle, sweating, and bleeding associated with winning. Do not join the frightened. In retrospect, there's very little more important in your entrepreneurial decision-making – should I or shouldn't I start a new business depends on the perfect season mindset – *zero-tolerance for losing.*

∞

Chapter 39
If you think you have the will-to-win, go deeper.

No business owner will ever last without a legitimate will-to-win. However, simply saying you have it isn't enough. Prove it. That's easier said than done because the will-to-win is often confused with the desire to feel the pleasure of the destination but not feeling the pain of the journey. The true will-to-win is not the wish to experience the joy of the final score. The true will-to-win is not the thrill of the moment where the reward is awarded. The true will-to-win is the *willingness to spill your guts* day-in and day-out without complaining, whining, rationalizing, irrationalizing, making excuses, pointing fingers, and looking for every escape from getting it done. The true will-to-win is commitment to the training...the journey. The true will-to-win is uncompromised dedication to the true leader of winning – work. A passion for the *work leading to winning* is the true will-to-win. A blue-collar tireless work ethic that won't accept mediocrity or failure. The promise of no compromise.

The concepts of winning, and will-to-win are often lost in translation. I've heard thousands of times, *"Coach, I want to win real bad."* Prove it. The *"will to win"* the *"passion to win"* and the *"desire to win"* are all empty words. They're just an arrangement of letters stuck together for entertainment and to give empty motivation for those desperate for a big win. They're an attempt to fill emptiness with more of the same. The reason for the emptiness of language is the *reality* void, that is, the absence of truth. Words alone are meaningless. Simply saying you have the will-to-win has no power, no force, and no ability to make it happen. Words alone are not even a goal or objective. Words gain meaning when *they light fire and move people.* When the actual first step is taken, then words take shape.

What's the best evidence of a will-to-win? Passing expectations. *Outcome passing income.* Working beyond expected output, doing your best when you hate what you're doing, and never having to wait or search for external motivation because the heat inside is your incentive. Anyone can be a star when you love what you're doing and when you're loved for doing it. The true mark of the will-to-win is shining in the dark. Spilling your guts off the stage, away from the spotlight and isolated from the applause. When the work behind-the-scenes becomes the real reward, you've proven that you have the will-to-win.

The true will-to-win is found by taking a close look inside and finding out whether you've got a track record of *over-delivering when you can't stand what you're doing.* What's your exchange rate? Do you consistently give more work than you've been paid for? Do you work on par? Do you work at a deficit as an underachiever who takes income without any outcome? Before you break away from your job and become a business owner, find out the truth about yourself. Have you respected other people's money? Did you truly earn every dollar that people gave you? Did you pass expectations? *What was the outcome of your income?* Did you give more or receive more?

Why is this important for entrepreneurship? Because the *habit* of passing expectations is a secret to recruiting and retention. Attracting customers and keeping them. Two separate concepts. Attracting customers is brutally challenging. Keeping customers is even tougher. Recruiting and retention are separate but connected complex dynamics with one common base: the meeting of expectations. Whether or not expectations are met determines customer arrival and departure. Habitually passing expectations becomes part of your business's brand...so does habitually failing to pass expectations. The habit starts long before you open the doors to your new business. It starts when you worked for other people.

- If you habitually cheated your employer out of expected work, you will cheat customers out of habit.
- If your income habitually exceeded your outcome, you will cheat customers out of habit.
- If you don't pass customer expectation, you will lose them and never attract more.
- If you habitually passed expectations at your job, your E-soul was in-training.

- If your outcome habitually exceeded your income, you built up your E-soul to go out on its own.
- If your exchange rate fluctuates wildly above and below the line of expectations, your E-soul is erratic.

Never start a business unless your E-soul has a healthy exchange rate. Make sure you habitually give more than you receive.

If you're not winning, it's because you're focusing on it. Wrong focus – you're focusing on the outcome instead of the job that has to be done. If your primary focus is not the job that must be done, you will replace its significance and never respect its relevance. In other words, you will make the actual job obscure. That's the reason why so many fall short of winning – tunnel vision; narrow-mindedness on the final outcome, which is the victory. Here's the reality check: winning is a by-product, not the focus. The trophy is the wrong focus. The focus has to be on how to get there – the job, the struggle, the training, and the practice. The blood, sweat, and tears have to be the reward. The trophy, the ring, the medal, and the belt are only symbols; not the true reward. Making the work the reward guarantees that you won't quit after the first loss because you will need the inner reward of doing the work.

Even though the focus on winning won't lead to winning, it's sexier than the truth. The will-to-win and all the work, sacrifice, sweat, and blood sounds too much like hell, so we shift our attention to the prize. However, winning the prize is not the big picture; it's just a close-up shot that leaves out the most important part of the story. True winning is not a single moment in time. True winning is a collection of sacred moments during which guts were spilled. It's easy for sacred moments to get lost in obscurity because the road to the actual prize is too long, too tough, and far too demanding. Without changing the perspective toward the journey, it will abruptly end. Why? Because when the journey has no meaning, it's dropped. The drive will end.

This is why winning is misunderstood. Winning is much more than numbers on the scoreboard. The true will-to-win will buckle the competition because the true will-to-win intimidates the opposition by proving, without a shadow of a doubt, that you will never back down, you will never quit, you will never lay off the pressure, and you will never stop no matter how mismatched you are.

Focus on the job, not the win. Not vice-versa.

∞

Chapter 40
Repeating a message.

You won't get it!

When the process loses its purpose, the journey isn't a reward.
When the only inner reward is winning, you won't get it.
When the only pleasure is the awarding of the trophy, you won't get it.
When the only rush is the ring, you won't get it.
When the only thrill is the winner's speech, the glory, and the adulation, you won't get it.
When your only focus is winning, you won't get it.

You won't get it unless you change your focus.

When you change your focus to the job at hand, you'll get it.
When you change your passion to the work, you'll get it.
When you feel the rush of blood, sweat, and tears, you'll get it.
When the inner reward is spilling your guts, you'll get it.

∞

Chapter 41
Pay to perform and perform to get paid.

"What are you trying to prove?" and *"You have nothing to prove."* are part of the conventional wisdom mythology that, on the surface, is intended to straighten you out. But all it does is kill your fire…if you let it. If you listen. If you let people make you feel guilty for having something to prove. If you let people make you feel crazy for admitting to it.

If you truly have nothing to prove, don't start a business. That's the best advice I can give you. It's one of the top five statements in this book. If you having nothing to prove, you will prove nothing, you will fail miserably, no one will take you seriously, you will end up in dead last, and, eventually, you will drop out of sight.

Every new business is started with the intention to prove something. No exceptions. Never believe anyone who tells you that s/he started a business with nothing to prove. A business is a statement – *I intend to prove I can make an impact on your life.* Every self-generated business is an assertion; a public declaration that announces it intends to survive by proving it can deliver what the public needs. Not wants, but needs. Every assertion is the equivalent of throwing down the gauntlet. It's a challenge to prove five points:

1. Prove you can deliver.
2. Prove you can cut it.
3. Prove you can be trusted.
4. Prove you're the best.
5. Prove you should be the one selected by the customer.

The essence of every business known to wo/mankind is *proving something.*

In order to prove something, an entrepreneur has to do something that no one else in the world has to do – *pay to work.* Then they have to out-work everyone to get paid. Business owners are the only people in the world who have to invest money to do their job. They are the only ones who have to shell out money to do what others get paid to do. Never forget the severity of starting your own business; you have to pay to get paid. Pay in money, and then follow by paying with your continuous, sustained top-level work. That's a lot to prove.

If you have the need to prove something, you don't need an X-ray, and you don't need an M.R.I. You positively have the E-soul. E-souls have even *more* to prove to themselves and to the public because no profession asks you to put up money to prove what you can do, and no profession asks you to prove more to get paid. Pay to perform and perform to get paid. You have to operate on a different temperature to not let that type of pressure crush you to pieces. You need a soul on fire – a scorcher. The power of having to prove something over and over just to survive has a special force; it ignites a blazing inferno deep inside your guts like nothing else.

However, the need to prove something is not enough. Do you have the willingness and capacity to *prove it?*

∞

Chapter 42
S/he who asserts must prove.

That sign changed my life and continues to deeply influence everything I do. A finger pointing at the reader with *"S/he who asserts must prove."* in bold letters below it. I read that sign for the first time on October 27, 1975, in the swearing-in room of the police station at the age of 18 years and three months. *"Remember it. Never forget it. It'll stop you from fucking-up."* The desk sergeant was right. It was a secret to success and failure, winning losing, messing up and cleaning up messes. Prove it. If you make a statement, prove it. If you want credibility, prove it. If you claim to be the best, prove it. If you mean what you say, prove it. If you want people to believe you, prove it. If you want customers, prove it. If you think you can do something, prove it.

The best way to make anyone believe, including yourself, is to *build a case*...a mountainous case. Build up mounds of evidence and present it in waves. Swarm them with overwhelming proof. Then, stockpile some more hardcore evidence and throw more bombs. If you want to become a full-time business owner, the biggest doubter in your product, your service, your staff, and your own competence will be you. Left unchecked, others will follow your lead. If you doubt your capacity to start a business and make it survive and thrive, no one will argue. Never expect believers to follow a skeptic. If you fear the worst about your ability, others will believe you and won't try to change your mind. Before you make the critical error of starting a business while you're engulfed in worry and anxiety, build up your self-belief with an overwhelming case that you can use in the future to convince your staff and potential customers that you know what you're doing and that you will be around for a long time. Proving your longevity is key. Prove your staying power. Prove your stamina and endurance. Prove that you are a machine, an unstoppable force that won't cave in at the first sign of pressure. *You have to prove your credibility.* Don't expect others to prove it on their own, or to yourself, or to anyone else. The onus is on you.

Your capacity to assert and prove has to be in place before your business kicks off. It has to be the starting point in proving beyond any shadow of a doubt that you have the soul of an entrepreneur. To bring out your E-soul, bring out the evidence. Baseless opinions are worthless. Zero evidence, zero value. Just *thinking* you can be a business owner is not enough. Warm and fuzzy thoughts of being your own boss, by themselves, prove nothing. Wanting to be your own boss proves only one thing – you're miserable. Deep down, you're not happy with what you're doing. You're unhappy with your current position. You're unhappy with how things are working out or not working out. Otherwise, *wanting proves nothing.* Performance is the universal language of proof. What have you done to believe you can do something new?

The most difficult person to convince with hardcore proof will not be your customers, your staff, your suppliers, and your bank. It's you. Start with yourself. Don't leave it to chance. Build your case. Make yourself a hardcore believer before the business starts for real.

∞

Chapter 43
Owner without an interview.

A terrible mistake you can make is to automatically hire and award yourself the title of business owner. Don't be a fool like me and automatically hire yourself as a business owner without any interview and without a shred of evidence that proves you are the right person for the job. No competition for your position of business owner is the height of favouritism, nepotism, and bias. It's unfair and flat out dangerous.

Before you debate whether to put president or C.E.O. on your brand new business card, interview yourself. Find out if you're qualified. Or, at least have the basics to build on. Don't do what I did – I never considered anyone for the job, never had a selection process, never even subjected myself to one of the useless, routine Q & As that decide whether to pay a stranger off the street millions for thirty years and then beyond into official retirement. I have sat on the questioning side of the table asking abject stupidity – *"Give us an example of a time when you had to inspire a large group of people."* – for about an hour, writing down a score, and then handing out a potential six-figure union-protected job that affected the minds of our next generation of gun-carrying cops…without ever checking if the answer was accurate or even the truth. I've seen late-night talk-show hosts get more meaningful answers from their guests. However, I never subjected myself to any questions, any scrutiny, any examination, and not even a second-thought.

If I had to do it all over again, I would start off with a level one interview. The basics. Just to find out if I had the raw materials. Here are the interview questions I would ask myself:

Introduction: You're going to be asked 50 questions. Answer each one with extensive, concrete narratives; not with abstract vague generalities or one-liners. Prove each answer with sworn eyewitness statements, affidavits under oath, physical evidence, and/or electronic evidence. Tell us *all* your experiences, not just one isolated example:

1. Explain your past experience in functioning without the security of a fixed salary, without union protection, without the guarantees of a collective bargaining agreement, and without the threat of losing your entire income for being incompetent.
2. Describe how you have beat insurmountable odds in the past.
3. Give examples of how you have stood up to the pressure of going broke without breaking.
4. What experience do you have turning around a lost-cause losing program into a winner?
5. Give examples of your ability to put out major fires on a daily basis that can bankrupt you.
6. Have you ever fought a Goliath? Have you ever called one out?
7. What's the biggest fight you've been in?
8. Explain in detail how you have made an impact on the lives of others. How did you do it? How often? To how many?
9. What's your winning record?
10. What's your formula for winning?
11. Explain how you have developed people and teams from scratch.
12. Explain how you reacted to your worst losses.
13. Explain your best examples of how you have investigated a colossal defeat and what lessons you learned.
14. Explain in detail your biggest miracle comebacks.
15. Have you ever accepted losing without trying to correct it?
16. How do you prepare and train a team to endure the struggle associated with winning?
17. Explain your biggest wins and exactly how you earned them.
18. Explain your past exchange rate. Give examples of how you have passed work expectations in the past.
19. Have you ever cheated your employer out of expected work performance?
20. Have your outcomes consistently exceeded your income? Give examples.
21. Explain your best example of excelling at something that you didn't like to do.

22. Explain your best example of working at peak performance without supervision.

23. What are your five biggest achievements?

24. Explain your best example of how you relied on your inner motivation to work through an intense struggle.

25. Explain, with as many examples as you can think of, where you gave more value than you received.

26. Have you ever had difficulty completing a task because it was too hard, or too time-consuming, or too far away from social life? If so, what was the outcome? Did you correct it? And, if you did, how?

27. Do you view work as pain or pleasure?

28. What strategy have you used to convince a team to buy into your philosophy and your system?

29. When have you ever had to convince 1,000 people annually to give you money for doing something they hate doing, like working out?

30. When have you had to convince 100,000 people to do what they hate, like read textbooks?

31. What strategies have you used to stop people from leaving your gym after they've paid you once?

32. How have you convinced people to choose your book out of the hundreds of thousands written annually?

33. How have you hired a staff to work for minimum wage?

34. How have you motivated minimum wage workers to clean toilets consistently?

35. Explain your full experience in training a minimum wage staff to sell memberships to skeptical customers who don't trust new businesses or the entire fitness industry.

36. Give us an example of a system that you have personally developed and executed in the past.

37. What are your strategies for selling H.E.L.L. in hell?

38. What is your personal brand?

39. Give examples of how you have taught customer service strategies to new staff members.

40. Give examples of how you solved conflict before it spread and infected your team.

41. What experience do you have in coaching, mentoring, and training a team to reach its peak potential?

42. Give examples of your willingness and capacity to build long-term relationships.

43. Give examples of your willingness and capacity to make long-term commitment.

44. What has been your experience in building a promotional campaign?

45. Explain how you have built teams from scratch to produce consistent quality performance.

46. Give your best examples of how you have made rapid-fire decisions without time to consult and research.

47. What experience do you have in fixing chronic team laziness that threatened the survival of your team?

48. Have you had your pay cut in half after you double the amount of hours worked? If so, how did you react? Did you run from the problem or fight through it?

49. What would you do if a customer harassed and threatened a pregnant woman on your staff?

50. Why do you want to be a business owner?

These fifty questions are just the first interview; a warm-up. Questions #1-49 paint a picture. The context. A level one contextual analysis would have saved me grief because:

- I would have understood the job of being business owner better by re-framing and re-defining it from a different perspective.
- It would have set the right focus to do my job as a business owner.
- I would not have underestimated the magnitude of being a business owner.

The last question is powerful. Question #50 has a different scoring system – it's a separate game. The answer is a win-or-lose score, nothing in between. You have to read it carefully and answer exactly what was asked. The question is not, *"Why do you want to invest in a new business?"* or *"Why do you want to work in a new business?"* The question asks for the *reason*, the *motivating* force behind your desire to be a business owner.

I'll start off with the wrong answer: *"I want to be my own boss."* Zero points. Lost the interview. Automatic fail. Two reasons why: first, if you want to be the *boss* of anything without earning it, you will fail miserably. Like with any boss title, it has to be earned. Otherwise, you will be incompetent. Starting a business for the sole purpose of *wanting* to be a boss is a knee-jerk reaction to being pissed-off at your current boss and/or former bosses. That's an acceptable *factor*, but it's not a *valid reason,* because it doesn't make you qualified. Secondly, a business owner is more than being your own boss. You have to be other people's boss. Separate concept. Not everyone has the balls or the maturity to be the boss, because being the boss means making the tough calls, making the obvious calls, getting out of the way, letting qualified people make the call, and knowing when to have that happen. Timing. That's the most difficult part of any type of leadership – play-calling. Knowing what call to make, who should make it, and exactly when. There's no cookie-cutter template, but there is a secret – develop a high Reality IQ, the potent combination of intuition and instinct; street smarts developed from years of practical real-life experience. There's no straight line to top-notch reality IQ; just a long unpredictable journey and a rough road you have to travel. The rougher the better. Soft ride, soft mind. Rough ride, tough mind.

What's the right answer? There's isn't a generic, read-from-the-card correct answer. However, there are two key elements to getting top marks. First, to answer why you want to be a business owner, define what a business owner means to you. Conceptualize it for your reality. Here's what I've learned in retrospect: a business owner is the face of the program. The head coach, not the player. The head coach puts it together and makes it happen. S/he makes sure that the system is built, that the right people are put in the right position, and that the plays are drawn up, expertly taught, repped out, and executed as close to perfection as humanly possible. The head coach calls the plays until it's time to hand it off. A business owner can't effectively be a player and a head coach. Player-coaches end up not doing either job very well. Secondly, you have to speak from the heart. Your answer has to be customized to match your personalized E-soul…your own one-of-a-kind, honest-to-goodness *brand*. Don't try to use someone else's answers. Don't try to say what you want to hear. Dig deep and bare your soul. Here's the answer I would have said if I had interviewed myself:

"I want to be a business owner because:
- *I am terrified of being bored to death. I need constant challenges. I need to compete – first with myself, then with the best in the business.*
- *I'm addicted to the thrill of doing what others think is scary, to beating the odds, to doing what people say can't be done, and to making positive ground-shaking impacts on as many lives as possible, especially the lost-causes and the social outcasts who have not been allowed to fit in. I don't want to bungie jump off a bridge, I don't want to skydive. I don't want to do any of the conventional "bucket list" superficial temporary band-aids that momentarily stop the bleeding of a meaningless life. If it doesn't make an impact on the world, I don't want or need a fleeting amusement-park thrill-ride moment.*
- *I need to be in total control of my potential. I can't have my gifts and talents buried by some egocentric manager who exacts revenge on the same level as miffed elementary-schoolers who leave you off their birthday party invitation list.*
- *I want to make a big difference by being as different as possible."*

Be a tough marker. Don't get soft. Don't be an enabler. Don't do yourself any false favours by handing out sympathy marks. Hiring or firing yourself is the biggest decision that will affect the survival of your business. Don't make excuses. If you're nervous, you should be. This is serious business. It's not a casual social chat. If you can't stand up to the pressure of answering a few questions about the person you should know inside-out, you'll shatter the first time your business starts bleeding. The evidence will prove if you're the right wo/man for the job. If not, don't do what incompetent organizations do: hire somebody just to get it over with. If you're unqualified, don't hire yourself as business owner. Don't get pissed off, just get better. Then, re-apply.

∞

Chapter 44
Hire yourself has a triple meaning.

Hire yourself is a multi-dimensional concept that will save your business if you apply all three meanings. The first has been explained – put yourself through hell to hire yourself. Secondly, save the questions and the process for future hiring, because *you set the standard.* Every staff member you hire on your team has to replicate *hiring yourself.* Your entire team must have the same core values as you, or at least the potential to have them and then develop them. This doesn't mean hiring and training clones. Far from it. It means hiring and developing a team that reflects your ideology about work and what it takes to win in the real-world. It means hire *conscientious* people. That's a key to survival. *Conscientiousness* is the one trait that guarantees winning and success by whatever definitions you give them because conscientiousness ensures that the team has, or can learn, every single characteristic and value to win big.

Thirdly, *hire yourself* means you have an obligation to your business to grow and *reach higher levels of consciousness.* Businesses have to grow and mature or they die. It's impossible to survive and thrive without getting built to last at full-strength. Raising your level of consciousness is a specific type of self-improvement where you elevate your awareness, which promotes transformation in your entire business, starting with self before spreading to the team and then to customers. *Reaching higher* is not just a catchy-phrase that makes for a good wall poster in your office. It's a pre-requisite for business survival.

∞

Chapter 45

Public sector is the worst training ground for the soul of an entrepreneur.

"If this were a private business, we'd be broke a long time ago." Common cliché that I heard in two public sector organizations over and over.

I'm not a public sector *job*-basher. I'm a public-sector *organizational* critic. Public sector jobs have 100% of my respect and admiration. It takes a certain set to save lives physically and intellectually. It's the organizations I have a problem with. They don't bring out your very best. They don't expect it, and they don't get it – literally and figuratively. I used to have a favourite saying that I bled to death at meeting after meeting: *"If we all get fired, we have no hope of surviving on our own."* Although it was intended as an insult, the common response I got was, *"Don't worry, nobody gets fired."*

A ruthless Darwinism is what makes private business different from public sector. Business Darwinism will kill off weak, immature businesses that don't, won't, or can't grow to full strength. Business Darwinism refuses to let the weak survive. It won't happen. The 90-10 mortality rate is the best evidence of an industrial-strength business Darwinism that simply won't let the weak get to the next-level. However, the weak can survive and thrive in the public sector. The reason is because the public sector is PR-rated – *protection and guaranteed.* Income is guaranteed to the organization, guaranteed to its employees, and jobs are protected by unions.

The difference between public sector leaders and private business owners is the *pay-for-pay investment.* No one person in any public sector organization makes a personal financial investment into the organization to get paid. No public sector administrator risks personal money to generate income. Public sector management never has to jeopardize every dollar they personally own for the organization's survival. Public sector doesn't have to put their financial future on the line. Public sector doesn't have to earn money. It's

217

handed money from an investment firm called *the government*, another organization who doesn't have anyone working in it who risks their own personal finances. Public sector and the government play with other people's money, not theirs. Without risking your own money, without the safety net of guaranteed income, it is impossible to experience the true depth, meaning, and consequence of entrepreneurism. It's impossible to *feel* it. If you can't feel it, you can't learn it. You can't become an expert at it. That's why there is no such thing as a true business leader in the public sector. A true business leader has to be a self-defence expert; protecting one's self from going broke. If you personally have no risk of going broke, you're not a true business leader. You simply work *in* a business. Therein lays a true challenge: how do you get authentic self-defence training? How do you prepare for the job of business owner?

Public sector *jobs* are a goldmine of life experience; a depth of wealth that will enrich mind, body, and soul. However, public sector *organizations* can bankrupt your mind, body, and soul. My public sector jobs have the capacity to teach infinite transferable skills that can lift your reality IQ score past your bodyweight. My public sector jobs taught me street-smarts that no level of education could ever match. However, the workplaces were also capable of pushing your IQ off a cliff.

True entrepreneurism starts with growing some and showing some. However, balls are not created equal. You can grow a sturdy set to do your job, but professional balls will not guarantee entrepreneurial balls. Here are some examples: I never once had a problem rushing to a 911 call. I never had a problem being the first to run into a crime-in-progress. I never had a problem making the tough calls during a football game. I never ran away from any workout. Despite all this, I can't explain the feeling the first time I was told my business was on the verge of bankruptcy. When your business is bleeding to death, you feel its pain. That's why public sector is the worst place for E-soul training. It doesn't teach you how to fight through the bloodshed of business Darwinism. When you fuck-up in public sector, you still get paid, but in business you get blown-up.

I have never worked in a public-sector meritocracy. The only true meritocracy I've experienced is sports and business. A meritocracy rewards performance in direct proportion with the level of accomplishment achieved. There's nowhere to hide. In both sports and business, there's a direct relationship between quality of reps and winning. Training and success are tied together. There's no other secret.

There's no training ground that prepares you perfectly to be a business owner. The E-soul can be developed in a wide range of experiences, but you can't become an expert until you actually do it for a long time. On-the-job training plays a big factor, but business Darwinism won't wait forever. Be careful if you work in the public sector. Public sector jobs may teach you skills and street smarts, but the organizational design will give you a false sense of security. Public sector and private businesses don't share the same reality.

∞

Chapter 46
Killing the clock is the worst regret.

I'm confident I could win, or at least contend for first place in, any contest about the most warped workplace stories. My first draft of this series included several examples as proof. The purpose was not to impress, not to vent, and not to whine; the purpose was to share evidence as a cautionary tale about the future consequences of workplace hell if you're stuck in one right now. I wanted to admit wasting an enormous chunk of my life poisoning my mind with idle gossip, pettiness, and adolescent conflict that sent me back in time to elementary school recess. However, I cut out the majority of workplace hell stories because the book became encyclopedic, and it caused genre-confusion – I couldn't tell if it was horror, science fiction, drama, mystery, or comedy. Instead, I chose to use them for a pilot of a television series that will make *The Office* look like a drama.

I have never believed in the *"I have no regrets."* myth. I'm conditioned to think *"bullshit."* every time I hear someone say it. Policing flooded me with skepticism because I experienced the 90-10 rule – 90% of what I heard was lies. Suspects lied, witnesses lied, victims lied, colleagues lied, and bosses lied. The 90-10 rule repeated itself during college teaching and coaching football. I don't believe anyone who says *"I have no regrets."* unless they prove it with hardcore evidence.

I live with major regrets about my professional life, specifically the amount of time I killed off the clock. I can't calculate the number of minutes and hours I wasted in workplaces that were environmental hazards, where toxic waste and air pollution threatened every fibre of my mind, body, and soul. Wasting that kind of life time is the equivalent of killing the clock, the bizarre strategy of intentionally letting the clock wind down to zero to protect a lead instead of playing the game full-out trying to score and give the fans their money's worth. Killing the clock is the chicken way out. Killing the clock is a manifestation of a gripping fear that has won the battle over your mind. Killing the clock is the saddest type of playing-it-safe, that is, watching the countdown rather than going for a big play, or even *trying* to run another play…any play. That's why fans boo when it happens. It's a rip-off. Killing the clock by watching time count down to zero, waiting idly for a wretched game to end, is a sad commentary on the clock-killer's state of mind – no self-confidence, no self-respect, no drive, and no ambition to give it your all while the clock's running. The only people who applaud killing the clock are the frightened; those who have let fear control their thoughts, their actions, their purpose, their potential, their destiny…and their life.

My examples of clock-killing workplace nightmares could fill another book…or an e-reader's entire memory. So I removed them. They're absurdities; a source of deep embarrassment for me to admit that it took me as long as I did to leave them behind. My workplace examples are dark, depressing stories of people dressed as grown-ups, getting paid as grown-ups, having grown-up titles but without the burden of behaving as grown-ups. Professional day-care.

I've tried to find a bright side. I've learned more about how *not* to destroy a team and organization than any MBA. could possibly have taught me. Here's a couple:

- *Unresolved workplace conflict* is the self-destruction of any team – sports, business, public sector. Unresolved conflict is organizational tobacco. Crack cocaine. It's addictive, messes up minds, and costs the organization a fortune in lost potential, lost minds, broken-hearts, and repairs. Unresolved workplace conflict needs a surgeon-general warning because it will attack every fibre of your health – physically, mentally, emotionally, and spiritually. It's impossible to gather humans in any place without the potential for conflict, but the wo/man in charge *has to solve it* a.s.a.p.
- *Letting it slide* is an organizational plague. Building teams is never easy. Getting to first place is hell; staying there is worse. The difference between first place and last place is *how much you let slide.* Letting it slide is the number one sign of leadership incompetence. Ignoring mediocrity, ineptitude, and outright incompetence is the worst form of

leadership negligence. You can't call plays when no one knows the plays. However, calling the plays is a piece of cake when everyone is executing. Firing on all cylinders is hard to stop. The type of machine your team becomes depends on how much or how little you let slide.

Here's my *theory of the causes of workplace conflict:*

- *Compensation for incompetence.* When people are out of their league and haven't got the balls to admit it, they compensate by acting. Drama. Suspense. Horror. All of which leads to comedy.
- *Meaningless job.* Conflict fills emptiness when the will or capacity to find meaning in a job is lost. More leadership negligence – a smart leader points out the meaning or injects some.
- *Boredom.* Fighting is exciting to those who cannot find stimulation in work.
- *Underdeveloped adult traits.* Immaturity is blind – it can't see the time wasted in conflict, because a personality stuck in high school or lower finds conflict entertaining. Refusal to leave adolescence sticks the mind in an emotional holding pattern.
- *Failure of character.* Weak conscience and weak work ethic. Time spent in workplace conflict is salary-stealing. The money should be forfeited as restitution for the crime of robbing the organization.

Why did I put up with a workplace that I held in contempt? Why did I kill the clock instead of trying to make bigger plays? Three reasons:

1. High pain tolerance.
2. Fight/flight switch stuck on fight.
3. Conditioning.

Beware of a high pain-tolerance. It has a bright side and a dark side. Iron-will is paradoxical. The ability to withstand misery can be a blessing or a curse. Pushing aside agony can push you to the next level, separating you from the rest, or it can stick you in the same place right smack in the middle of the pack. Mental toughness can make you strong enough to fight through meaningful adversity, or it can weaken you by fighting through meaningless adversity. A key is *picking your fights carefully.* It's the difference between growing and stagnating. It's the difference between getting built and building cobwebs. Meaningful fights build you up. Meaningless fights tear you down. The true challenge is telling them apart. I failed miserably. I thought a meaningless fight was meaningful. That was wishful thinking. This type of colossal blunder happens when you're desperate to find meaning in a workplace that has become meaningless. Lowering your pain tolerance is the key to walking away from hell and leaving misery behind. The more pain you tolerate, the more time you waste.

The reason we have a fight and flight switch is to save ourselves. Picking the right one at the right time is crucial for survival. Getting it wrong will cost you your life – professional life or real life. I stayed in a workplace hell because my switch broke. It got stuck on "fight". If my switch was functional, I would have taken flight long before I did. Check your switch regularly. Make sure it's functional. A surefire sign of the broken switch is the one-sidedness. If all you're doing is fighting conflict, it's time to check the switch. Lop-sidedness is not normal. You need a balance between fighting and fleeing. Contrary to what I used to believe, I can't change the entire world. There are certain workplaces that you can't change, because change has to come from within. If the combatants don't want to change, there's nothing to fight about.

I was raised to be thankful for any job, regardless of where it ranked on the scale of traditional social importance. I had it hammered into my head that every job is important. I was taught to find meaning in the work itself, never to complain, never to whine, and absolutely never to embarrass myself with the irresponsibility of *quitting.* My parents lived through unimaginable poverty, war, and depression. I knew that I was blessed with a level of profession-al comfort that they would never enjoy. Thus, my pain tolerance skyrocketed. If they could survive the depths of hell, surely I could handle a few assholes. I never lost sight of my blessings, and never stopped giving thanks – to a fault. Conditioning obscured calling. Every thought of leaving a career turned me into a punching bag for my conscience. Quitting a respectable job was cultural treason and heresy. My solution was to dramatically change my perspective.

First, I changed how I viewed the concept of *quitting a job*. I never quit a job. I quit organizations. I quit workplaces.

Secondly, I re-framed the decision from *quit to answering a higher calling*. Higher callings are not optional. I don't believe that every calling has to suit our liking. Our higher calling doesn't always fit our wants; they fit needs and other people's needs. Higher callings are not intended to make our lives struggle-free. They're intended to give us purpose and meaning by making it happen in the big picture, whether we see them or not. It's up to us to open hearts so we can open our eyes. Our higher calling fits in a grand scheme that's out of our league to fully understand, but we can learn to see how the pieces fit in a small corner of the big picture. I learned that it's easy to underestimate the full impact of our higher calling. We may not see or feel any impact at the moment, but the spread effect is powerful – what we do and don't do with our higher calling spreads farther than the naked eye.

Thirdly, I re-defined quitting as *giving up because it's too hard.* I presented enough evidence to myself to prove that wasn't the case. I built my case that I handled everything my jobs threw at me. I reversed my perspective – to grow some and show what I had to accept a new challenge; a bigger, stronger challenge that I was unfamiliar with. Finding something else that's hard to do is not quitting – it's growing. Stepping into the *discomfort zone* of unfamiliarity and uncertainty forces you to take a *heart test*. Do you have the heart to find something inside that you didn't know you had? It's part of the self-evolution. Changing careers needs a big set. It's not quitting when it's growing some and showing some.

Fourth, I acknowledged the concept and power of the *performance demand.* I believe that a new assignment isn't a choice. There's no option and no escape. You can fight it or flee from it, but it always catches up to you. I learned that leaving a career is neither irresponsible nor quitting, because it's a performance demand to move to the next-level.

How is a performance demand made? How do you know for certain that you're being told to move on to the next assignment? How can you be sure that you're not being impulsive and making a regrettable mistake? In my case, the same tactic was used – my play-calling was taken away. When my first public sector job ran its course, after fighting and fleeing from the next call, an asshole appeared in my life. Like a bad joke. An asshole from the past was moved into my way for a purpose; to take away my most prized professional possession: play-calling. The same thing happened in my second public sector job and that was the breaking-point. The threshold. The no-brainer decision was to leave. It happened naturally and it felt natural. Both decisions were peaceful – a deep sense of inner peace before the official decision was made. That's how I knew – *peace of mind without having to give anyone a piece of my mind.*

I fixed the switch; it was no longer jammed on "fight". Many life decisions are not cut and dried, but these were. That's the power of a performance demand. The force of reaching the threshold position is a next-level moment, lifting your level of consciousness through sticking points that kill the clock.

∞

Chapter 47
A secret to peace of mind is clock management.

If you call a lot of slow, boring plays, don't expect to score a lot. If you want to eat up the clock with safe run-of-the-mill plays, don't be upset when you don't light up the scoreboard. When you get stopped dead in your tracks, don't be outraged when someone else puts the ball in the air over and over, and goes for it all the time. Don't be jealous or envious of those who score more points. How you move the ball is your choice...so is how often you find the end zone. If you don't cross the goal-line enough, don't blame the refs, the environment, the climate, the fans, the other team, or your team. Blame your play-calling. Blame your coaching. Blame your practices. Blame your training. Blame yourself for putting a half-assed mediocre product on the field. Blame yourself for being a lousy coach.

Manage the clock wisely. How you manage the clock today will determine how you view the past – as a blessing or a curse:

- Whether you get stuck in the past or free yourself from it.
- Whether you live in the past or learn from it.
- Whether you repeat the past or defeat it.
- Whether you escape from hell or keep burning in it.
- Use every moment to go deep.
- Call for big plays.
- Expect big plays and big plays will happen.

∞

Chapter 48
What's it like to lose your title?

After I left my jobs, my popularity grew. I have two theories why: first, the magic of *missing*. There's a strong tendency to miss what you had when you no longer have it. People will miss you more when they think they're missing out on what you're not missing. We have a tendency to romanticize the past through the magic of selective memory. The script is easy to change from non-fiction to fiction. Secondly, I represented *certainty*. I could give free consultation about the after-life; life after the job that people cling to with dear life.

"What's it like?" Three words that scare the shit out of people who want to leave their jobs...or have to leave them. Translation: what's it like to *lose your title?* The title is the fight for your mind. You get awarded the title in exchange for your mind, heart...and soul. I've been blessed with titles that people make movies about, but titles are temporary. They're not permanent. Be careful when you lose it because losing the title can make you lose your mind unless you have the right perspective of the after-life – life after losing the title. The main reason people crack up after losing the title is because most define themselves by the title instead of the actual work performance. Defining yourself with a title is basing your identity on that title. When the title is gone, so is the identity... and the mind follows. Loss of identity is too much to handle for a weak mind which has no work performance as evidence to back-up the identity asserted by the title. Titles are superficial. Performance goes deep. Reversing it is the true threat to your mind. A reversal is too heavy of a burden to carry.

A key issue is experience – did you experience enough before you resigned? Did you experience what you should have with your title? Did you experience the max – the fullest? If you've lived a full, rich career, you'll be fine. In my case, I had enough evidence that I had experienced the max with each public sector title. In addition to the evidence, there's a feeling that will back up the evidence – a feeling of being tired and unmotivated. A fatigue that comes from having emptied the tank at the same level you're plugging away at with no re-fueling. No charging the batteries with newness; new challenges, new scenery, new environment, and new experiences. When new experiences stop, you know you've maxed out your title.

Here's a checklist of secrets that will help you survive the afterlife of losing your title:

- *Never define yourself by a title while you have the title.* Don't carry the title 24-7-365. Don't introduce yourself while off-duty by title, rank, or job description. Give yourself a break from your title and build-up your true identity by introducing yourself as something other than your job, e.g – spouse, partner, parent, sibling, and any other interest other than your job (*"Hi. I work-out. Pleasure to meet you."*). The biggest mistake you can make is defining yourself solely by a title because when you lose it, you'll lose *it*. Your title is not who you are. You give meaning to your title, not vice-versa. Define yourself by the totality of your performance personally and professionally. You are what you do physically, intellectually, emotionally, and spiritually, not what is printed under your name on a business card. A title is not an achievement, not a reward, and not an award. It's an obligation and a responsibility that you earned. The true reward is how well you fulfilled your obligation. You can lose your title, but your will never lose what you did with it.

- *Never believe you were stripped of the title.* If you believe you've been stripped of a title, you will feel naked. Your title is not armour. It's not a shield. It's not protective equipment. It's not bullet-proof. A title is not a possession, but it will *always be part of your brand.* If the title was stripped, change the language immediately. Personally, I can't stand the phrase, *"Get over it,"* because it's a typical scolding cop-out – telling someone the outcome, but not having the decency or the intellect to say how exactly. *Teach me!* If you want me to get over something, show me how. Teach me the way. Here's how you do it – *change the focus.* Shift your attention away from the hurt and the pain to the *thrill of the next challenge.* Search for it. Find it. The search itself is a challenge. *Past hurt can push you, not sink you.* Re-wire your switches. Don't run from the uncertainty of new challenges. Fight through them. Never forget that a past title is a permanent part of your brand. A title can only be stripped from the present and future, but not the past. The past is etched in stone. So is your title.

- *Never believe you lost the title fight.* Some titles are lost during a battle. Never take it personally, and never make it personal. It is impossible to lose a title fight, because the title can only be passed on to someone else. Titles are never truly lost; they're handed down. You can't lose the past; you can only brand it. *How you brand the past will determine your future.* If you did lose the fight for your title, you still won, because *nothing just happens.* Study losing, and you will find the secret to winning. *You have to lose before you can win*[16]. What this really means is losing needs a different perspective. Re-define it. Losing is not a failure unless you fail to investigate it and learn how to change it. Losing is simply a problem-solving exercise, and an opportunity that was given to you to move on to the next level.

- *Never say, "Those were the best days of my life."* At a faculty meeting, I heard one of the dumbest, most dangerous statements I have ever heard. A professor informed the room that students are told that college is the "best days of their lives." Then, I heard an assistant football coach say the same asinine statement to players. I repeatedly told students and players otherwise, because it's not true. Imagine having the best years behind you at the age of 20. Imagine having the best years behind you at any age. What's there to look forward to? What can you aspire to in the future if the best days are in the past? Same applies with jobs. Never say that your best

---

16   Tribute to a masterpiece, Dream On. Aerosmith and Steve Tyler.

days were in a job that you're leaving or will leave someday. Never attach the label "best days" to anything in the past, because the past was just a warm-up. Your "best days" are in the future. If you don't believe that, you're heading for darkness.

- *Never use the word "retirement."* The word retirement should be abolished from the dictionary. It's a personal culture shock that is capable of scarring your psyche. Retirement causes a mental knock-down, capable of leaving you with a psychological concussion and long-term lingering symptoms that make you feel different than who you were. If you want to avoid depression, feelings of inadequacy, meaninglessness, insignificance, and irrelevance...don't retire. Change your perspective by changing your language. Here are two examples: change careers, and move to the next level. This language will keep the motor running. It won't leave you with the question: Is this it? Asking that question has a bright side and a dark side. *Is this it?* is a challenge. If you can't solve it, you're in trouble. If you answer "yes", you're on a dark road. If you answer "no", you flipped the right switch.

- *Earn more titles.* This is the big one. This is the top secret to handling the loss of a title. Earning more titles injects purpose and meaning. It will force you to do *roadwork*, an intensive training program that will divert your attention from all the potential darkness, depression, and dread of unresolved inner conflict brought on by a title loss. *Earning more titles means moving up in weight class.* It means moving up into the heavyweight classes. Fight Goliaths. Call the beast and call out your inner beast. A retired title-holder is a sympathy-drawing has-been who gets soft and mushy while searching for cardigans, rocking chairs, and 15% discounts while re-telling "remember-when" tear-jerkers. As long as you train for another shot at the title, you won't lose your mind. The search for the next-level will help the potential crash from a high-level to point-zero. There's a big drop from a top-level to doing absolutely nothing. Be careful of slamming on the brakes. Abruptly going from sixty to zero can snap your head back.

If you make a past title the highlight of your life, you are doomed to a low-light life.
Never believe the highlight is over because, if you never have something to look forward to, you'll always look back.
If you always look back, you'll never see what's in front of you.
If you never see what in front of you, you'll crash or go past it.
If you crash or go past it, you'll miss it.
If you miss it too much, you'll miss the opportunity to grow.
If you miss the opportunity to grow, you'll miss your next calling.
If you miss your next calling, someone loses out.
They'll lose out on what you're supposed to be and what you're supposed to do.

The fight for your mind starts with what you're willing to fight for. Working for someone else has a purpose – you get money in exchange for spilling your guts and the privilege of practical experience. You're given an opportunity to learn what you can never learn in a classroom. However, gut-spilling is paradoxical. Spilling your guts has a value. Profit is made from the guts you spill. Eventually, you open your eyes and see that if you spill your guts for your own business, the reward will be bigger.

Change your perspective. Change your inner dialogue. Like with any title, the title of business owner is sacred. Once you hire yourself, respect the title. Spill your guts. Fulfill your obligation. *Defend the title.* After you hire yourself, people will downplay what you do. Statements will be made that will make you question yourself and potentially fill you with self-doubt. Here are two recent examples of never-ending tests that challenge your title:

"Do you still own that gym?" – the equivalent of asking, *"Do you still have kids?"*

"The biggest mistake you made was quitting the police. You should go back." – the equivalent of saying, *"You should never have left hell. You should go back to hell."* And the person telling me this was a retired business owner.

These statements exceed arrogance and exceed ignorance. The reason why people will degrade your title of business owner is brainwashing. They fell into the trap. They lost their minds. They believe that the only title worth having is one given by someone else.

∞

Chapter 49
A self-generated business can save lives.

If you want to be a business owner, and are trying to make a decision but your confidence or even business is shot, think of this: if you stick it out, your business can save lives.

My businesses save lives, but I had no idea they had life-saving potential at first. Life-saving wasn't my top priority when I started my businesses. I didn't even think of it, because I only learned conventional bullshit about what a business was supposed to be. Read a conventional business plan, and there's no box to tick off for *life-saving* as a goal. However, the Law of Unintended Consequences took over. Over a decade later, lives were saved. Here's what my businesses did:

- Rescued me from the depths of madness; from a burning hell that words alone cannot explain where I was wasting my talents in a place that awarded minimal effort as much as maximum. My businesses reversed the aging process. I returned to fighting shape physically, intellectually, emotionally, and spiritually.

- Rescued my wife from working 16 hours a day managing an unmanageable transportation company. She was strapped in a losing battle to make someone else rich. Another anti-aging miracle. Our businesses allowed her to follow her calling as a business leader and publishing editor.

- Rescued my oldest daughter from burying her talent sitting behind a desk in a bank directing traffic. Our gym allowed her to follow her calling as a fitness coach, who consistently makes impacts on lives every day, and as an entrepreneur, who started a thriving boot camp business from scratch.

- Rescued my second daughter from burying her talent babysitting a nuthouse-workplace for an incompetent business 7 days a week, allowing her to follow her calling as a book publisher and an entrepreneur who started a photography business from scratch.

- Rescued my son-in-law from a sinking company, allowing him to become the gym coordinator and a full-time dad.
- Rescued my granddaughter from never having to be raised by day-care, nannies, or total strangers.
- Let me pour my heart and soul into my granddaughter instead of spilling my guts trying to put out fires in a flaming hell.
- It's where my third daughter met her husband.

Here's a different perspective: if I had caved in to fear and never opened my businesses, my family's lives would be in an unthinkable hell controlled by other people who would be living our current lives. Even though our businesses have yet to make a financial fortune, we amassed an I.Q.-fortune – **I**ndependence **Q**uality-of-life fortune. I.Q. has replaced the conventional, limiting *goodwill* value. It's impossible to place a value on the independent quality of life that our businesses have provided. That's an incalculable fortune. I re-defined rich a long time ago. The businesses' bank account is the obvious scoreboard that controls our I.Q., but the scoreboard of life has a completely different set of dynamics. We've endured struggles that were impossible to predict when we opened for business. A key is sticking to it by never losing sight of the true value of a business – the I.Q. The I.Q. became our driving force; the impetus to meet every challenge and fight through them

If you decide to start a business, you'll never regret it if you keep your eyes on raising the I.Q. If you have a business already, and you're questioning yourself, doubting yourself, and beating yourself up; re-define rich and you'll realize your fortune. Never forget the I.Q. and you'll be guaranteed with the fire to stick to it. Once you reach a life-altering IQ-level, it will be impossible to ever go back to working for someone else.

∞

Enjoy the book?
We would like to hear from you.

Post a review on Amazon, Goodreads or let us know directly at
reviews@ginoarcaro.com.

Follow Gino on Social Media

GinoArcaro

@Gino_Arcaro

+GinoArcaro

GinoArcaro

Gino's Blog

Follow Jordan Publications Inc. on Social Media
for up-to-the-minute information on Gino and his books

GinoArcaro.Author

@JordanPubInc

+GinoArcaroBooks

More Books by Gino Arcaro

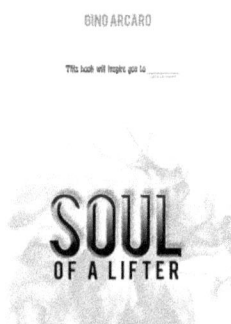

Soul of a Lifter

Gino Arcaro's journey from childhood obesity to natural health and strength was not made alone; he relied on the Soul of a Lifter. In telling this tale, Arcaro draws on life lessons learned from his careers as a football coach, police officer and college teacher to inspire and lead the reader in a soul-searching quest to reach his/her own potential. This is not your run-of-the-mill motivational book. Discover insights about what drives the soul... what happens when you listen and when you don't!

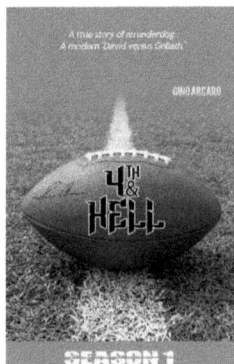

4th & Hell Season 1

"We were David with a Canadian passport, failing miserably at winning just one football game against stars-and-stripes-draped Goliaths." It came down to fourth and hell – a face-to-face showdown. No disguises, no masks, no secret weapons. No one huddled on the sideline. No one huddled on the field. Both sides knew what to expect. No surprises, no guess-work, no mind games. Making the call was a formality. All that mattered was running the play to see what would pass. Someone would execute; someone would be executed.

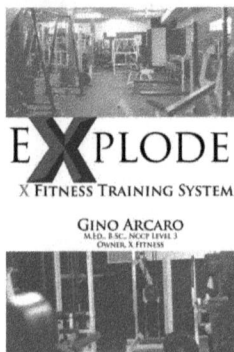

eXplode: X Fitness Training System

Sought after his entire adult life to help others achieve their workout goals, Arcaro put his weight lifting theories and routines into this manual. His "Case Studies," true stories from his 40+ years of working out (completely natural) bring a sense of reality to the average gym-goer who just wants to get in shape, stay in shape, and most-importantly, not quit. No gimmicks, just discussion and formulas that can be tailored to any situation regardless of how long or how intensely one has been working out.

True Confessions

Gino Arcaro relates and upholds a simple fact: "Everyone has a conscience. No exceptions. If you're alive, you have a conscience. The myth of 'no conscience' actually means 'weak or dysfunctional' conscience." Therefore, a truth-seeker must appeal to the conscience, meaning, "make the conscience work out, make it work right, and make it do all the work." True Confessions is a manual for anyone whose job it is to get the truth. For example, Human Resources personnel during the job interview process or Law Enforcement interviewers who can use Arcaro's theories to open a window into the psyche of a suspect under interrogation.

Fat Losing: The psychology of fat fighting
"Waste Mis-management leads to Waist Mis-management"

This is not a diet book. This 40-page eBook explains the most important truth about fighting fat: it begins at the top – literally. Without a proper mindset, no amount of dieting or counting calories will workout. Digesting Fat Losing is the first step to understanding how to change your habits and thinking for once and for all. It contains practical discussions that engage the reader in re-thinking the obstacles that stand in the way of becoming a healthier person. Gino Arcaro, a self-proclaimed "dysfunctional 12-year-old, trying to overcome my obesity," is an expert on the subject. He's written Fat Losing to share what he has learned and practiced for over 40 years.

Be Fit Don't Quit

Full of exercise ideas young children can try on their own or with a parent, this book will rekindle in any adult a love for the simple act of playing. Gino Arcaro has spent his life working out and teaching young adults about the importance of "being fit." He wrote Be Fit Don't Quit to express a tried-and-true message: Exercising is natural and fun. Never quit!

SWAT Offense

By connecting partial concepts that can build any formation, any pass play and any running play to fit the situation, at the line of scrimmage, Arcaro has designed a system that eliminates the need for a conventional playbook that has to be memorized. Memorization is replaced by translation of a simple language. He designed the SWAT offense as a solution to a nightmarish reality of limitations – poor talent and poor resources, a one-man coaching staff, open-admission players, and on top of it all, out-matched opponents…willingly sought out! David constantly calling out Goliath. Arcaro's SWAT offense is the most unique offensive system you'll ever see because it has limitless offense capacity but no playbook. A unique feature of the SWAT Offense is its ties to SWAT Defense.

SWAT Defense

Making the defensive call has never been harder. Coordinators have the greatest challenges in football history. Spread no-huddle offenses, extreme passing, clock-changing rules. More to defend, less time to think. Arcaro's SWAT Defense shows how to beat the spread by forcing the offense to go deep and crack under pressure. "A stress-filled workplace for quarterbacks and receivers leads to an explosion." Central to Arcaro's system is his decision-making model that teaches defensive coordinators and players to make the right calls – those split-second decisions that have to be made about 60 times per game. Making the right call is not easy. Like any skill, defensive decision-makers need guidelines and experience to develop into full potential. A unique feature of the SWAT Defense is its ties to Arcaro's SWAT Offense.

For more free book previews or to purchase Gino's books go to
WWW.GINOARCARO.COM

.

www.ingramcontent.com/pod-product-compliance
Lightning Source LLC
Chambersburg PA
CBHW032302210326
41520CB00047B/862